MARATHONING
Start to Finish

by
Patti and Warren Finke

Illustrated
by
Clive Davies

Copyright (c) 1986, wY'east Consulting
All Rights Reserved

Published by wY'east Consulting
6917 S.W. 33rd, Portland, Oregon, 97219

Cover Photo: 14th Annual Portland Marathon
by Yukihiko Yamaoki

Editorial Assistance: Richard Busby

Printed in the United States of America

ISBN 0-9616865-0-2

CONTENTS

Introduction 1

Starting Out 3

Training Principles 9
    Marathon Physiology 10
    Keys to Success 15

Base Building 25
    Plans, Paces and Progressions 26
    Getting Out the Door 35

Sharpening 39
    Maximizing Performance 40
    Psychological Preparation 50
    Peaking 55

Race Preparation 59
    Race Preparation 60
    Planning Your Race 67

Racing 75

Recovery 87

Aids to Performance 95
    Supplemental Training 96
    Food and Performance 122
    Ergogenic Aids 137
    Running in Temperature Extremes 142

Appendices 151

Index 181

Terrific! This book is an inspiration. It is without question the most comprehensive marathon training guide that has been published. Patti and Warren Finke make you think about what you are doing, tell you how to improve and, at the same time, allow you to enjoy the challenge of running a marathon. Whether an experienced marathoner, a middle-of-the-pack runner, or a beginner, this book is well worth reading.

Les Smith
Director, ORRC Portland Marathon

INTRODUCTION

The marathon race has been traced to 776 BC and the races held at the ancient Greek Olympic Games. The games came to an end in 349 AD when the Christian Emperor of Rome banned the Olympic Festival as a relic of paganism. In the following centuries, the glorious deeds of the athletes and the noble spirit of the Olympic competition were not forgotten.

The father of the modern Olympics was Baron Pierre de Coubertin, who dreamed of an athletic competition worthy of the name Olympics that would bring together the best athletes of all nations of the world for a series of contests dedicated to the highest ideals of amateurism, brotherhood and peace. In 1894 Coubertin arranged a meeting of representatives of dozens of nations and the International Olympic Committee was formed to stage the first Olympics of the modern age to be held in Athens in the spring of 1896. One of the events to be included was a race designed to retrace the steps of the Greek soldier who in 490 BC, after helping the Athenians trounce the invading Persians at the Battle of Marathon, ran 25 miles from Marathon to Athens to proclaim the news. When he arrived he gasped "Rejoice we have conquered", then died on the spot. This event was recorded by the Greek historian Herodotus who did not identify the runner.

On April 10, 1896, 25 runners heard the gun go off at Marathon for the Olympic race and started the 25 mile course over rock strewn roads. More than 60,000 spectators were in the Athens stadium and another 60,000 were on the hills watching the games and waiting for the marathoners to arrive. The favored Greek runners were well off the pace for the first half of the race, but one, Spiridon Loues, steadily moved up through the slowing pack starting at about the 15 mile point. He caught the leader, the Australian Flack. They raced side by side until Flack collapsed at mile 23. With the stadium in sight, Loues ran down a path cleared by the police through a crowd that was showering him with flower petals. The Greek spectators went wild with enthusiasm as their runner won the race. This race was the beginning of the modern marathon. The marathon has been an event in each Olympics since then and in 1984 included a women's race for the first time. The official distance was changed to 26 miles 385 yards at the London Olympics in 1908. The extra distance was added so that the royal family could watch the start from Windsor Castle. The first American marathon was sponsored by the Boston Athletic Association in 1897 and the event has grown tremendously ever since.

From Start to Finish

Every marathon starts long before the runners merge behind the starting line waiting for the gun to go off. A commitment by the runner to do the actual training required to cover the miles is the real beginning. The marathon does not finish when the runner crosses the line. It finishes only after the runner recovers, is able to enjoy the magnitude of his/her accomplishment and is motivated to set new running goals.

This book approaches marathoning with an emphasis on efficiency of training and prevention of injury. The training program described is one that the authors have developed and used personally over the almost 10 years they have been running and competing. It combines thousands of miles of trial and error experience and the results of the latest exercise physiology research. (Predictably, exercise physiology reinforced what the authors had, for the most part, learned the hard way.) The program is the philosophical basis of the Portland Marathon Clinic, a 6 month series of lectures and training runs co-directed by the authors (Patti and Warren) and Bob Williams. The main goal of this book and the Clinic is to make the marathon experience as rewarding and enjoyable as possible for all participants, whether novice or seasoned veterans.

STARTING OUT

STARTING OUT

How can you determine if you are ready to start training for the marathon? Marathoning is not for the beginning runner. You should have been running for at least 6 months and be running over 20 miles per week if you want to run a marathon 6 months from now. If you already have a good mileage base or have run previous marathons, then you're definitely ready to begin a training program designed to help you reach your top performance.

You should already have a good level of fitness and have consulted with your physician concerning any medical problems. The training programs described in this book are conservative with emphasis on injury prevention and adequate rest.

We heartily concur with the recommendation of the American Academy of Pediatrics that children before puberty should not run the marathon. We've seen too many children suffer psychological burnout and physical problems to feel otherwise.

There is no difference in marathon training between men and women except when women are pregnant. Fitness running (30 minutes, 3 times/week) has been shown to be beneficial for pregnant women; more exercise than this may be harmful to the baby.

Are there special considerations for the older runner? We are both in our 40's and feel we have long years of competitive running ahead of us. Clive Davies, a friend and this book's illustrator, is now over 70 and still sets age groups records at the marathon and lesser distances. Studies of middle aged marathoners showed that they compared favorably with runners in their 20's in high aerobic capacity, high efficiency of energy, low percentage of body fat and ability to exercise at a high percentage of their aerobic capacity. The current world best for the marathon was run by Carlos Lopes at age 38.

However, as you get older, you may find that you need more time to recover. You may have to run fewer miles and run those miles at a slower pace. Supplemental and cross training may also be more important.

Goal Setting

The first step in any program is to define goals. The term goals is used in the plural sense because a series of goals should be set: long, medium and short range. A long range goal may be to finish your first marathon, or to improve your time from a previous marathon best. Shorter term goals may include running several 20 mile training runs and increasing your weekly training mileage.

The value of goals results from the fact that the higher standards you set for yourself, the higher your attainment. The setting of performance goals does not in itself produce achievement. The motivational effect of goal setting most likely results from self-reinforcement. After the goal has been set, self-approval is based on reaching that goal which makes you work harder to keep from disappointing yourself. Once goal performance has been achieved, you are no longer content and then make self reward contingent on progressively more difficult accomplishments. Motivation then results from seeking out and conquering challenges and achieving goals which are optimal for you, neither too difficult nor too easy.

Commitment

The setting of goals must be accompanied by commitment. In life, to excel you must use your abilities to the fullest capacity. To excel in the marathon, you must be physically and psychologically fit. You must believe in your own capabilities and fully commit yourself to their fullest development. Commitment is a major key to the psychological attributes necessary for excellence. Peak performance comes from assuming active responsibility for your own success. We can show you the necessary tools, but you must use them. The level of your commitment to the marathon is your choice.

Volition or willpower is the core of the self. Willpower decides what is to be done, applies the means to do the task and persists in the task in the face of all obstacles. Learn to identify volition by identifying your personal needs and the experiences that strengthen you. Volition affects mental performance, thoughts, feelings and physical parameters such as strength, responsiveness and the desire to succeed.

A part of commitment is "mission" or your personal reasons for pursuing a particular goal. While your goal may be to finish, your mission may be to be in command of your body and push it to its limits.

Outlining A Plan

One way to help achieve a day to day level of commitment is to formulate a plan and keep track of your progress. Start now by writing down your long range goal (i.e. running the marathon in some time). In the following chapters we'll show you what medium range goals (training milestones) will support this. If you follow the points set out here, you will be able to devise a week by week, day by day training plan. This technique will yield

a systematic approach to achieving your long term goal via a series of small and achievable steps leading from where you are now to to where you want to go. Each step can be used to assess progress toward the long term goal.

TRAINING PRINCIPLES

MARATHON PHYSIOLOGY

Physiologic principles and adaptations form the basis for marathon training requirements. There are two basic principles which underlie all types of athletic training: overload and specificity.

Overload

Overload means exercising at a level which causes the body to make specific adaptations to function more efficiently. Overload does not mean overtraining. Think of a rubberband - as more pull is applied it stretches more and becomes easier to stretch, but too much pull can cause it to snap. To keep the runner from breaking, i.e., becoming injured or ill, overload must always be used in conjunction with rest. Overload and rest form the basis for what is known as the "hard/easy" training approach. This technique uses variations in frequency, intensity and duration to achieve cycles of overload and rest. Frequency is how often you run, intensity is the pace at which the workout is conducted and duration is the time spent on an individual run. In a program of increasing mileage or of building basic endurance, "hard" may be a long slow run while "easy" may be a shorter distance run at the same effort. For the experienced runner with an established mileage base, "hard" might be a shorter workout of increased intensity such as hill work, fartlek or some kind of interval training. After a hard workout, rest or an easy workout is important because it allows the muscles and other tissues a chance to rebuild and adapt to the stress. This is the basis of overload training.

Specificity

Specificity refers to adaptations of both metabolic and physiologic systems, depending on the type of overload used. Specific exercise brings about changes in those systems used in that particular exercise. Running is obviously the specific training for running. Different adaptations result from different kinds of running using variations of frequency, intensity, duration and terrain to utilize different sources of energy. This is where long term goal setting is so important: you need a running program designed for the specific type of races you want to run. This approach will assist you to maximize performance and eliminate wasted effort. Specific endurance training with its resultant physiologic adaptations is essential for marathons.

Energy Sources

Energy to perform work comes from the generation of a substance called ATP, (adenosine triphosphate). The breakdown of the food provides the sources of this energy. The main energy sources used in endurance running are carbohydrates, (stored in the body as glycogen), and fat. When these materials are broken down in the presence of oxygen, the metabolism or energy used is termed aerobic. The waste products of this aerobic metabolism are water (H_2O) and carbon dioxide (CO_2). Metabolism is termed anaerobic when the glycogen is broken down to form pyruvate and, lacking oxygen, further breaks down into lactic acid.

The body can endure only limited amounts of lactic acid. If lactic acid accumulates, fatigue occurs faster and glycogen breaks down rapidly, depleting your energy source. Anaerobic metabolism provides energy for short intense exercise such as sprinting or for bursts of speed in sports like soccer and basketball. In prolonged exercise, the major metabolic pathway used is the aerobic one. When aerobic metabolism cannot meet the requirements for energy due to either increased intensity or prolonged time, anaerobic metabolism may be called in for short term assistance.

Carbohydrates are the most readily available source of energy in the muscle and are utilized mainly in faster continuous running, especially for shorter distances. Fat is the major supplier of energy at slower paces or for longer distances. More oxygen is required to produce an equal amount of energy when fat rather than glycogen is used as the energy source. In addition fat requires some breakdown of carbohydrates to be taking place simultaneously. The body can not accumulate adequate glycogen stores to provide enough energy for the duration of the marathon. Many marathoners have experienced a severe energy loss around the 20 mile point in a marathon. The effect is referred to affectionately as "Hitting the Wall". Hitting the wall is thought to be the depletion of muscle glycogen. Fat stores (even in the leanest runners) are almost inexhaustible. However, when muscle glycogen is gone, fat is probably unable to be used because it needs some carbohydrate as a primer for its metabolism.

Marathon Requirements

Running the marathon requires a combination of both carbohydrate and fat metabolism. The physiologic goals of a marathon training program are to provide enough endurance training to optimize aerobic metabolism; to have the ability to metabolize fat while running faster paces and to facilitate increased storage of carbohydrates.

These goals require adaptations to allow greater consumption and utilization of oxygen. Some of these changes occur at the local muscle level and include better utilization of oxygen through increased size and number of mitochondria (little energy factories within the cells) and an increase in their aerobic enzymes. These muscles can more easily mobilize and use fat for energy, which helps to preserve the carbohydrate stores. The body also develops a greater ability to store and utilize carbohydrates. Some muscle fibers can be adapted for aerobic or anaerobic metabolism exercise. For the marathon, you want to adapt these convertible muscles for aerobic or endurance work. Through training there will be an increase in the number of capillaries for better nutrient supply as well as an increase in the amount of muscle tissue.

Adaptations of the cardiovascular and respiratory systems are also important results of training. The heart muscle increases in size and weight and the amount of blood increases. Resting and submaximal exercise heart rates are decreased. The amount of blood that the heart pumps, called the stroke volume, increases which aids in increasing the amount of oxygen that can be extracted from the blood through better distribution of blood to the working muscles. As the blood goes through the muscles, increased utilization of oxygen from the blood results in increased consumption of oxygen.

VO2 Max

One of the most important training adaptations is an increase in the maximal oxygen uptake, called VO2 Max, which is a quantitative measure of a person's capacity for aerobic energy transfer (the ability to do work). An improvement in VO2 Max thus increases the amount of work you can do, that is you can run faster and/or farther. Variables that determine VO2 Max are heredity, sex, body composition (the amount of lean body tissue), age and training. Obviously you can do nothing about several of these variables, but improvements of 20-25% in maximal oxygen uptake because of training have been observed. VO2 max peaks within 6 months to 2 years after starting an endurance training program. However, even after it has levelled off, it is still possible to improve performance. Typical marathoners are able to maintain their pace using approximately 75-80% of VO2 Max for the well over 2 hours required. Some athletes, notably ultramarathoners, are able to work for prolonged periods at levels approaching 90% of VO2 Max. The ability to run at higher percentages of VO2 Max may be explained by the concept of anaerobic threshold. Anaerobic threshold is the point when increasing intensity of exercise causes lactic acid to accumulate and impair performance. Improving the anaerobic threshold means that you can run harder for a longer period of time without going into anaerobic metabolism and accumulating much lactic acid. Studies have shown that anaerobic threshold can be increased by endurance training.

KEYS TO SUCCESS

One important measure of a successful training program in any sport is economy, "getting the most bang for your buck". Economy has two benefits: 1) you can achieve a higher level of training with the same outlay of effort and 2) the risk of injury is minimized or reduced. A successful training program employs all of the following keys:

- Hard/easy cycles

- Specificity

- Injury prevention techniques

Hard/easy Cycles

Training is accomplished by the adaptation to repeated stress. If overload or stress is repeated many times, it results in specific adaptation of the body in a way that will strengthen resistance to the stress. In running, stress can be applied by increased speed and/or distance. Adaptation does not take place during the overload or stress period, but during the recovery or rest periods between stresses. During stress microscopic cell destruction takes place and working muscles and cells are depleted of necessary enzymes and nutrients. During recovery periods, microscopic rebuilding takes place along with some overcompensation. This overcompensation is what is referred to as "training effect".

In a runner's training program, overload (hard workouts) can be achieved through either added speed or distance, while recovery takes place only when both speed and distance are minimized (easy workouts). To quantify these the following definitions are given:

- **HARD** : a workout in which the distance is greater than 20 percent of a runner's weekly mileage *or* a workout run at greater than 85% of the maximum pace the runner could run for that training distance.

- **EASY** : a workout in which the distance is less than 10 per cent of a runner's weekly mileage *and* is run at less than 80% of the maximum pace the runner could run for that training distance.

The more often you can overload and recover, the better. The key limitation is recovery. If the overload is too great, it may take so long to recover that you don't get the maximum number of overload/recovery cycles and you may get injured. If the recovery is inadequate, you will not have the strengthened resources to overload during the next cycle. This leads to injury.

Adequate recovery between overload cycles requires 48 hours or longer. Forty-eight hours is the minimum time needed to replenish enzymes and nutrients, such as glycogen, within the muscle cells after a hard workout. For this reason, most successful training programs have at least one easy workout day following each hard workout day to allow for recovery. An easy workout, in lieu of total rest, can actually help speed the recovery by increasing circulation to the recovering tissue which helps flush out wastes.

Specificity

Since adaptation to overload tends to respond to the specific stress involved, it follows that the stress should overload the muscles and other systems used in the activity for which you are training and that the stress should simulate the type of activity (i.e. aerobic, anaerobic, etc.) An economical training program therefore should be tailored to the type of activity for which you are training (ie., endurance running requires long duration runs for training as opposed to short sprints). A corollary to specificity is that the component parts of a sport can be trained for separately and specifically. This will be discussed later.

Injury Prevention Techniques

Any training is better than no training. Hence, the most important aspect of any training program is injury prevention. Useful strategies and tactics for doing this are:

- Having a training plan.

- Separating speed and distance.

- Allowing adequate recovery between hard workouts.

- Monitoring the response of your body to training.

- Utilizing coaches and clinics.

Training Plans

The best strategy is to devise and write down a training plan that has target times and distances which will stress, but not break the runner, and will allow adequate recovery between hard workouts. If the training is going to increase over the long term, (ie. building mileage or adding more speed work), this increase should be gradual, at a rate of 5% per week or less.

Once a training plan is established, it should be viewed as a flexible framework around and within which the runner can employ various tactics to lessen the risk of injury. These can include variations in terrain, surface and shoes. If necessary, individual workouts can be eliminated or changed or the overall plan can be modified.

Separating Speed and Distance

A key technique used in training is functionally specific workouts. These workouts concentrate on one element of the training at a time, independent of the other components being trained. This independent training is highly effective and allows one part of the body to rest while the other is trained, minimizing overuse injuries.

Specific elements of long distance running are speed, (aerobic power), and distance. These can be trained using workout combinations shown in the speed/distance matrix below.

Workout Effort

	DISTANCE		
	<10%	20%	30%
	Weekly Mileage		

SPEED		<10%	20%	30%
	75%	Easy	Hard	Very Hard
	80%			
	85%	Hard		
	90%			
	100%	Very Hard		

The filled in squares in the matrix effectively separate hard or very hard efforts in either speed or distance from their counterparts on the other axis and are recommended training techniques. A complete training program includes workouts that are speed specific and those that are distance specific.

Combinations of speed and distance, (blank squares in matrix), may be effective training techniques, but provide a much higher risk of injury because the total stress is higher.

For long distance runs, such as the marathon, 95% of all training should be specific to endurance. Hence, nearly all hard workouts should be either hard or very hard distance runs done at an easy speed. Speed training is used most effectively only during the final weeks before the event for sharpening or for periodic fitness measurement.

Recovery

In order to get the training benefit of hard workouts, there must be adequate recovery provided to let the body rebuild. The matrix below gives the number of recovery, (easy workout), days which are recommended following various workout efforts. Typical workout weeks employ 3 hard workouts alternated with 4 recovery days.

Recovery Days after Workouts

		DISTANCE	
	<10%	20%	30%
		Weekly Mileage	

SPEED		<10%	20%	30%
	75%	Easy	Hard	Very Hard
	80%	0	1	2
	85%	Hard		
	90%	1	3	5
	100%	Very Hard		
		2	5	8+

Note that we have included recommended recovery days for mixed speed and distance workouts. This can be used as a guide for those of you who overdo occasionally or run races (100% speed).

Self Monitoring

A very useful aid is a training diary where you can record your training plans and goals. You can note resting heart rate (HR), recovery HR, weight, daily and weekly mileage, times plus a general comment on how you feel each day. An example is shown in the Appendix. Learning how your body reacts to overload and when to rest is important in maintaining health. You can use monitored heart rates to monitor the result of effort of running and recovery. Heart rate recovery consists of two phases, short and long term. During the short term phase, the HR drops rapidly from the exercise rate to about 20 to 30 beats/minute above the resting HR. The long term phase may last for varying periods depending on the total stress of the run. Monitoring how long it takes for your HR to return to the resting rate is a good way to see whether a run has been too hard and a rest day is in order. Usually this long term period should be several hours, but it may last up to 24 hours after a long run. The guidelines for recovery time and HR are different for each individual. A diary can help you determine your particular normals and monitor yourself.

It is important to dispel the old myth "No pain, no gain". It is possible to train and improve by hard work that does not include pain. It is not possible to train at all if you are sick or injured. A good training program works to prevent these complications. Dick Brown, the former coach of Athletics West, felt that a major part of his role was to keep his athletes healthy. There is no one "right" way to train and each runner needs to learn how his or her body reacts to different overloads and what works best. But remember, *overtraining does not help anyone* and a rest day is definitely in order when there is:

- An increase in resting HR of 5 beats per minute or more

- A sudden weight loss of 5 or more pounds

- A feeling of excessive thirst

- A sluggish or very tired feeling

- The beginnings of illness such as sore throat or cough.

One good way to reduce the possibility of injury is to run as much of the weekly mileage as possible on soft surfaces. The soft surface transmits less shock to the body and protects the joints. The best plan is to do the long runs on dirt trails if available. Remember that training times on hilly trails will be a minute or more per mile slower than on the roads. Training times must be adjusted accordingly.

Some of the questions most commonly asked by runners involved in a training program are of the form "What happens if:

- I miss a day because of illness or injury?

- I need a rest day and my schedule calls for a hard day?

- I miss a whole week of training?

- My ... hurts, should I run on it?

The answer to all of these questions is "Learn to listen to your body and respond to it's needs!". If something is painful while you are running on it, that is your body's way of telling you that it is being abused. Heed its cry. Skipping a day or a week will not cause you to fall into immediate decay. Do not feel guilty, do not be compulsive, and do not add the missed workouts or mileage into your future schedule. If your body tells you it needs a rest, listen. The major goal is to remain healthy, injury free and enjoy your running, not to rack up as many miles and consecutive days as you can. If you have missed workouts, it may be necessary to drop back to an easier schedule for several days or weeks and then gradually return to the previous one. Remember, only you can hear your body protest and only you can do something about it.

Coaching and Clinics

In some cases, runners may benefit from outside coaching. A coach should have an unbiased view of cause/effect relationships and may be more likely to protect the runner from injury than the runner himself. Many running clubs have coaching available or can provide you with group training sessions and clinics where support and answers to your questions are available.

BASE BUILDING

PLANS, PACES, AND PROGRESSIONS

There are three phases to marathon training. The first phase is base building during which the runner builds the strength and endurance base necessary for specific marathon training. This phase may take 4 to 6 months for the beginning marathoner. The second phase is the sharpening phase which employs specific marathon workouts to achieve maximum marathon performance. This phase is usually 8 to 10 weeks. The last phase is the race preparation phase which encompasses final preparation, planning and resting during the week or so before the race. Twenty six week marathon training programs for beginning, intermediate and advanced marathoners are listed throughout the book to be used as examples.

Some Definitions

The specific endurance training requirements for a marathon are too demanding to be "done from scratch". The average runner who runs 20 to 30 miles per week would quickly break down if he attempted to do 20 mile marathon training runs because of the lack of an adequate base. To run long training runs, you must run enough miles to adequately prepare your body for the stresses involved.

What is adequate mileage base for a marathon? It depends on your goal and your body. If you are a beginner and your goal is to finish, you may do so on 45 miles per week if that training is very specific for the marathon. For experienced runners who want to achieve a good performance, we recommend a minimum of 60-65 miles per week. With a 65 mile a week base, you would easily be able to tolerate the 20 mile training runs and some specific "speed work" during the sharpening phase. Part of your training involves becoming attuned to your body and being able to judge how many miles your body will tolerate; how it will respond to the different training techniques and what is optimal for you.

Before going any further, we will reiterate some training terms in the context of building a mileage base. Later, as we get into the sharpening phase we will expand these definitions.

- **EASY** : a description of effort and can be used to describe the runs where rest and rebuilding occurs. Easy can either refer to pace or distance. "Easy" is a pace that is about 75 - 80% of the pace that the distance could be run in a race *and* a distance of 10% or less of the weekly mileage. Many runners do not realize the importance of easy runs and do not get adequate rest. The consequence of this is that they cannot get the benefits of hard runs because they are too fatigued. The body does not have a chance to rebuild in response to overload in such situations.

- **HARD** : also a description of effort and describes training when the principle of overload applies. Hard can also be defined in terms of distance or pace. During the base building phase, it refers to runs of longer mileage (more than 20% of the total weekly mileage) which are run at an "easy" pace (75-80% effort). In the sharpening phase, hard workouts will use increased intensity or pace.

Charts of "easy" paces (75-80% effort) are given in the Appendix for runners of different abilities.

Building Endurance

The basic training for all distance racing is endurance training. The runner must have the stamina to cover the desired distance. Cardiovascular endurance comes first. Then the specific muscles become stronger, followed by the connective tissues, tendons and ligaments. Injury often occurs because the runner wrongly feels that he has the stamina to run the required number of miles, but actually lacks the muscular and connective tissue strength which develops much more slowly. Base building for the marathon should follow a schedule designed to build mileage slowly and comfortably to the level where your body can tolerate the necessary long training runs.

During the base building phase, a general scheme of workouts over a 7 day (weekly) period might look something like this:

Day	1	2	3	4	5	6	7
Normalized Distance	3	1	1	2	1	2	1

The normalized distances are based on the hard runs being either 2 or 3 times the distance of the easy runs. All of the runs are done ar any easy (75-80%) effort. This results in maximum improvements in aerobic metabolism which lead to increased aerobic enzyme production, better fat utilization and adaption of convertible muscle to aerobic use. There are three "hard" runs per week and 4 easy recovery runs. One of the hard runs is particularly long and is followed by two recovery days. Most runners refer to this workout as their "long run" of the week. It is the basis for their endurance training. *The ultimate goal of the base building phase is to slowly build up the length of your daily runs to the point where the long run simulates the endurance requirements of the marathon.*

Beginning

Many runners will start marathon training from schedules that are low in total miles, do not reflect a hard/easy structure and do not support 7 days a week of running. The first improvement to be made is to adopt the hard/easy approach to training. The easy days may, in fact, be days of no running at all or may mean playing golf or bicycling. But you must have hard days for overload and easy days for recovery to get maximum benefit from training.

More advanced runners with higher weekly mileage should also examine their weekly workouts to see if hard/easy cycles are being used. They may already be running a total mileage consistent with marathon training (8-9 miles/day), but not be completing long runs sufficient for proper marathon training requirements (20 miles or more). Base building in this group may not require running more miles per week as much as it may require slowly changing workouts to adapt to longer runs.

Pace

During the building phase, the primary goal is to develop endurance. Hence the emphasis for the hard runs should be on increased distance rather than speed (remember the matrix). Training at 75 - 80% of the pace you could run in a race of the same distance is an adequate speed to accomplish this. Pace charts are in the Appendix to help you decide how slowly you should be running. Other ways to tell if you are running at the proper pace are by perceived exertion and the "talk test". If you feel that you are working hard or that the pace will be difficult to maintain, slow down until the work level is easy or moderate. If you can not carry on a conversation with another runner or need to speak between gasps of air, slow down to what would be a conversational level. You can also monitor effort using training heart rates. The exercise heart rate is based on a calculated per cent of maximum HR. Find your maximum heart rate by subtracting your age from 220. Then, calculate 60 to 70% of your maximum. (Example age 40, 220-40=180, 0.60x180=108, 0.70x180=126. A forty year old's easy training heart rate should be between 108 and 126.) If you are increasing your mileage a great deal, you are getting all the stress or overload needed without doing any fast paced running. Be patient and stay healthy, speed will be developed later when your body has the strength to handle its increased demands.

Mileage Progressions

Once you have established a hard/easy routine in your training, you can begin to add mileage to build a base for

the marathon. Mileage increases should be no more than 5% per week. A hard/easy version of progression is to add 10% every two weeks. To increase mileage, first increase the length of your longer runs. Increase the length of your rest runs only when they are well below 10% of your weekly mileage. This will assure that you get maximum recovery. Plan your schedule to allow you to reach long runs of about 20 miles 8 to 10 weeks prior to the marathon. Exactly how long does the long run need to be for marathon performance? For the beginning marathoner, you need to run for about the same length of time as you will run during the marathon. This means about a 20 mile run, if you run it at the recommended 75 - 80% easy effort. The balance of your training may not support runs much longer than this with attempts at longer distance leading to injury or extreme fatigue. For those with more experience, especially those trying to improve performance, a few runs up to and possibly beyond the marathon distance could be valuable. Try to keep your schedule close to the *3:1:1:2:1:2:1* daily ratios discussed above.

Each workout should consist of at least a 5 minute warm-up, (a fast walk or slow jog), before the run and a five minute cool-down, (again a slow jog or walk), after the run. These can be incorporated into the training run by simply starting and finishing at a slower pace. Increased mileage makes a stretching program a necessity, especially for the muscles in the lower back and the entire back of the legs. A program of slow stretching should be done after the completion of the workout at least 3 times per week; stretching every day is recommended and more beneficial. A specific stretching program is described in the Supplemental Training Chapter.

Double Workouts

Some runners like to break up their longer mileage workout days into two runs. Endurance training benefits still are derived from this due to incomplete recovery between runs. However, the benefits are certainly not as great as from a single longer run. *Specificity* demands running 20+ mile runs if you want to train adequately for the marathon.

Racing

If you want to run short races during your marathon training program, you must weigh their importance against your marathon goal. Since a short race requires at least as much recovery as a long run, you should never do both in the same weekend (see the recovery chart in the Training Principles section). You are better off to replace your long run with the race and stay healthy rather than to try to maintain your weekly mileage. In so doing, you will lose the specific marathon training benefits of the long run and detract from any base building progression. Once you have an established mileage base, some racing may be helpful as a sharpening technique.

Example Programs

To assist you to devise a personal training program, several base building mileage progressions are given below. Remember to use the training pace charts given in the appendix to determine a target pace for your training runs.

Beginning Marathoner Basebuilding

Starting Point: Six months of running experience and a base of 20 miles per week.

Goals: Long term: To finish a marathon. Medium term: To build a base that will support some 20 mile training runs and some marathon specific speedwork during the sharpening phase (weeks 18-25).

Mileage Progression

Week	S	M	T	W	T	F	S	Total
1	6-8	0	2	4	2	4	0	18-20
2	7-8	0	2	4	2	4	0	19-20
3	8	0	2	4	2	4	0	20
4	9	0	2	4	2	4	0	21
5	10	0	2	4	2	4	0	22
6	10	0	2	5	2	5	0	24
7	10	2	2	5	2	5	0	26
8	11	2	2	5	2	5	0	27
9	12	0	3	6	3	6	0	30
10	13	0	3	6	3	6	0	31
11	14	0	3	6	3	6	0	32
12	15	2	3	6	3	6	0	35
13	16	2	3	6	3	6	0	36
14	16	2	3	8	3	8	0	38
15	18	0	3	8	4	7	0	40
16	16	2	3	8	4	8	0	41
17	20	2	3	8	4	8	0	45

All runs done at the 75 to 80 % pace. See pace charts in Appendix.

Intermediate Marathoner Basebuilding

Starting Point: Experienced runner, may have run one or more marathons; has a base of 35 to 40 miles per week

Goals: Long term: to improve marathon time by building better endurance and using more specific training. Medium term: to achieve an endurance base which will support 20 mile runs and some marathon specific speedwork during the shapening phase (weeks 18-25).

Mileage Progression

Week	S	M	T	W	T	F	S	Total
1	8	2	4	8	4	8	4	38
2	8	4	4	8	4	8	4	40
3	10	4	4	8	4	8	4	42
4	10	4	4	9	4	8	4	43
5	10	4	4	10	4	8	4	44
6	12	4	4	10	4	8	4	46
7	12	4	5	10	4	9	4	48
8	13	4	5	10	4	10	4	50
9	14	4	5	10	4	10	5	52
10	15	5	5	10	4	10	5	54
11	16	5	5	10	5	10	5	56
12	16	5	5	11	5	11	5	58
13	17	5	5	12	5	12	5	61
14	18	5	6	12	5	12	5	63
15	18	5	6	12	6	12	6	65
16	19	6	6	12	6	12	6	67
17	20	6	6	12	6	12	6	68

All runs are done at 75 to 80% pace. See pace charts in Appendix.

Advanced Marathoner Basebuilding

Starting Point: Experienced road racer, most likely with previous marathon experience; has a mileage base of 50 miles per week.

Goals: Long term: to improve marathon time by building extra endurance and speed. Medium term: to achieve a base which will support runs of marathon length and marathon specific speed work during the sharpening phase (weeks 18-25).

Mileage Progression

Week	S	M	T	W	T	F	S	Total
1	14	4	4	10	4	10	4	50
2	14	4	5	10	4	10	5	52
3	15	5	5	10	4	10	5	54
4	16	5	5	10	5	10	5	56
5	16	5	5	11	5	11	5	58
6	17	5	5	12	5	12	5	61
7	18	5	6	12	5	12	5	63
8	18	5	6	12	6	12	6	65
9	19	6	6	12	6	12	6	67
10	20	6	6	12*	6	12	6	64-68
11	22	6	6	12*	6	12	6	66-70
12	22	6	6	14*	6	12	6	66-72
13	24	6	6	14*	6	12	6	68-74
14	24	6	6	14*	6	14*	6	64-76
15	24	6	7	14*	7	14*	6	66-78
16	25	6	7	14*	7	14*	7	68-80
17	25	7	7	14*	7	14*	7	69-81

* Runs may be replaced with equivalent *speed workout* of about half the distance (See Sharpening). Otherwise, all workouts are at 75 to 80% pace. See pace charts in Appendix.

GETTING OUT THE DOOR

Sometimes the most difficult part of training, especially during the basebuilding period, is getting out the door to go run. This is true even for experienced highly competitive athletes. Most of them have little motivational "tricks" that work for them. Some of these helps are listed below. Writing down a planned workout schedule is the first place to start. You have then made a date with yourself to complete a series of workouts. Filling out the training diary and being able to check off or fill in the appropriate space often works as a reward. Seeing all those completed workouts certainly encourages you to keep on being able to fill the pages.

Goal setting is an aid to planning the workout schedule and a key motivator. To achieve your goals, you must go out and train. Achieving a goal motivates you to set a new one. Tell your family and friends some of your goals and ask for their support to help you meet them. Doing so is a commitment to your goal.

Call or arrange with a friend to meet you to run. You will feel obligated not to disappoint them and you may actually enjoy running with someone. If this idea works for you, plan weekly training sessions with others such as attending group runs. You can even go to a race and run at training pace if being with others is important to you.

Try to create a habit. Set aside a specific time to run and let everyone know that this is your time to run. If you're really having a hard time and can't tell if you're physically or really only mentally tired, try the 5 minute test. Tell yourself that you only need to run for 5 minutes. If you still feel terrible at the end of 5 minutes, quit and enjoy a rest day. Usually, since you're already out there and feeling better, you'll decide to complete the workout.

Give yourself rewards; have a beer or a cookie after running; plan a family activity after completing the week's schedule with their help. Buy yourself some new shoes or shorts for meeting your goal mileage base. Use whatever rewards appeal to you. Including your friends and family in the rewards also encourages them to be supportive of you and your goals. As you run more, it becomes addictive and you feel deprived if you don't do it. Often the running becomes its own intrinsic reward. Use the "Premack Principle". This involves making an activity that is usually done contingent on an activity you want to do. If you usually read the newspaper when you get home, make reading the paper depend on going out for your run first.

Incorporate variety, run a different course, try new shoes, call a new friend to run with you. Try to incorporate your running into your lifestyle. Run to work, then you'll need to get home somehow - run. Try running as a means of transportation at other times. Interest your family and friends in running so that you can run together and so they can understand your need to train. Be creative and enjoy your running.

When it is difficult to get out the door because you are sick or injured, listen to your body. Workout schedules are guidelines not requirements. It is always OK to skip a workout or take an easy day if your body or your mind needs the rest. You can train effectively only if you are healthy, so do all you can to stay that way.

SHARPENING

MAXIMIZING PERFORMANCE

The primary goal of marathon training is to build endurance. Inherent in this goal is the establishment of a sufficient mileage base. The mileage base is not an end to itself, however, but is the means for creating the stamina to support the real key to training - hard/easy cycles and in particular, the long run. As your base mileage and stamina build, you are able to do more work in your long runs and recover using longer easy runs. Without the base and the stamina, the long runs would provide a stress that you could not recover from, stopping you from doing the multiple overload/recovery cycles necessary for training. Once an adequate base has been established, you can improve marathon performance through sharpening.

Sharpening is an 8 to 10 week period during which very specific training is used. To do this training you must have built a base which will allow you to do vigorous marathon specific workouts without breaking down your body.

Sharpening Workouts

Sharpening workouts can be categorized as one of three types: Endurance, Pace or Strength. Beginning marathoners should concentrate on endurance while intermediate and advanced marathoners can benefit from pace and strength training.

Endurance

The key to the marathon is the long distance endurance run. During the sharpening phase, runners should do as many long runs as is practical, up to one per week. These runs should be done at an easy pace to encourage fat metabolism and must be long enough (approximately 20 miles), to fatigue the primary endurance muscle fibers and bring into play the convertible fibers which are not normally used. Aching upper leg muscles, especially outer quadriceps, at the conclusion of a long run, are a sure sign that you have run far enough to accomplish this.

Pace

The purpose of pace training is to attain neuromuscular coordination of the body at race speeds. This ensures maximum efficiency and conserves energy resulting in improved race performance. Pace training for the marathon is achieved by running short distances at goal race pace. An important side benefit is the development of pace judgment (being able to tell how fast you are running) so that you run "under control" during the race.

Strength

Strength training for distance runners seeks to improve aerobic capacity (VO2 Max). To do this, workouts are designed to stress anaerobic threshold by running at or, in some cases, beyond the threshold for short repeated bursts, or by running near maximal effort for longer continuous distances

Glossary of Mystifying Training Terms

All types of training can be categorized into the three types listed above. However, if you go to your local running club meeting or pick up a copy of a running magazine, you will find many mysterious terms for different forms of workouts. We have included some of these below along with other definitions. We apologize if we have left out anyone's favorite.

- **Speed Work** : a general term for almost any fast paced strength or pace training. An integral part of any of these types of workouts is at least 5-10 minutes of warm up and 5-10 minutes of cool-down.

- **Fartlek** : Swedish for "speed play" - a type of continuous training often run on hilly courses in which the runner speeds up or slows down at will or with the terrain. The runner might run faster for 30 seconds, then slow down for two minutes and repeat this sequence throughout the workout. (Strength Training)

- **Tempo Runs** : a short hard paced run. Typically it is run near race pace. (Pace Training)

- **Time Trial** : a time trial is used to measure progress and should be run at all out pace for the distance covered. An easy way to run a time trial is to run a short race, the distance of the race should be 10% or less of the weekly mileage to allow reasonable recovery. (Although not really training, it has strength training benefits)

- **Intervals** : repeated short periods of work followed by rest intervals of reduced activity. The work intervals are often run near maximum aerobic pace and are followed by intervals of recovery, usually to 60% of maximum heart rate. (Strength Training)

- **Repetition Running** : interval training run near race pace with full recovery to 50% of maximum heart rate. This type of running is very specific for leg speed. (Pace Training, Strength Training when high volume)

- **Maximum Heart Rate** : maximum heart rate in beats per minute can be estimated by subtracting your age from 220.

- **Maximum Aerobic Pace** : the fastest pace you can run aerobically. It is scientifically measured by treadmill testing, but can be determined using the 12 minute test. The 12 minute test is done on a track or measured course with the distance covered during a 12 minute run divided into the time to give maximum aerobic pace in minutes per mile. A simple mathematical calculation which gives a reasonable estimate for interval training is 2.2 times 10K time in minutes equals 440 time in seconds at maximum aerobic pace. (See pace tables in Appendix)

- **Hill Training** : does not mean simply running on hills, but is a specific hill technique. A hill with a gradual 5-10% grade that is 100-300 yards long is used. The runner repeatedly runs or bounds up the hill and strides down the hill as fast as possible (this should include 30-60 seconds of hard running). Uphill develops dynamic power and downhill develops rapid leg movement patterns and stride length. (Strength Training)

- **Even Effort** : a description of pacing best utilized on hilly courses. The best plan is to expend energy at a constant rate throughout the run. A common problem on hills is that the runner expends so much energy on the uphill that he/she cannot use the advantage of the downhill to run faster, but uses it to rest. A better plan is to run up and down the hills at the same effort, then using that effort on the downhill becomes a major advantage. Uphill is usually run about 10% slower than the flat while downhill is run 5% faster.

- **Cross Training** : training using other types of aerobic activity such as swimming or bicycling. The values of cross training are thought to be in terms of injury prevention. The aerobic endurance training may or may not be equivalent. The specificity component is missing. Part of cardiovascular endurance involves the training of the muscles used for better oxygen utilization through increased aerobic enzymes. This can be done somewhat through cross training, but specific training is better. Cross training will benefit you especially if you cannot run every day. It will add some variety and help keep you motivated to stay on your training schedule.

Interval Training

Interval training was developed by German physiologists in the 1930's and popularized by the great Hungarian coach Mihaly Igloi. There are 5 variables used in describing interval training:

- The fast run distance
- The recovery run distance
- The recovery run activity (slow run vs. walk)
- The time for the fast runs
- The number of repetitions.

Manipulating these variables makes interval training adaptable to virtually all types of running. Interval training can be applied very effectively to anaerobic running, sprints and middle distances. This is because it allows large amounts of anaerobic work to be done by interspersing it with recovery periods.

While training for long distance events where anaerobic demands are minimal and speed requirements are far below anaerobic threshold, the most suitable use of interval training is to improve aerobic power. The most effective way to do this is to repeat short fast runs close to maximal aerobic pace. This pace can be calculated by multiplying a runner's best 10K time by 2.2. This gives his maximum aerobic 400 meter time in seconds. Multiplying by 1.1 gives his 200 m. time. For example, if you run a 40 minute 10K, you should run your 400 meter intervals no faster than 40 x 2.2 = 88 seconds and your 200 meter intervals in 40 x 1.1 = 44 seconds. Because this maximal aerobic pace can only be maintained for approximately 12 minutes without stopping, fast run distances of much shorter duration allow a greater total work load to be completed. Most research indicates fast runs of 200 to 400 meters to be most effective for improving VO2 Max. Because the intent is to maintain the cardiovascular system near its maximum aerobic limit, rest intervals should be short, about 1/2 of the fast distance or less and should be run slowly rather than walked to decrease lactic acid buildup in the muscles. The runner's pulse rate should drop to about 60% of maximum during this rest period. The number of repetitions depends on the conditioning of the runner. A runner starting an interval program should begin with a total fast run duration of less than 12 minutes. This would be about 6-8 400's for most runners. As recovery pulse and leg fatigue indicate, more intervals can be added.

Tempo Runs

Tempo runs are runs done at constant moderate effort, usually at or slightly faster than race pace. These runs have two benefits. First, because they are run near race pace, they are effective physical and mental simulators of a race. The body and mind learn to function efficiently at racing speeds. The neuromuscular communication paths necessary to operate in a race are established. The runner's feel of racing speed is developed. A second benefit of tempo runs can be derived by running tempo runs at 85-90% effort. This creates a cardiovascular overload and accompanying strength benefits similar to those derived by aerobic interval training. Optimal tempo runs combine both of these effects through an educated selection of a tempo run distance of about 1/4 of the race distance. If this distance is run at race pace, it will always be a 85-90% effort run. For the marathon an excellent tempo run workout is 6-7 miles at marathon race pace. Because of their dual benefits, tempo runs are probably the most effective type of speedwork training for the marathon.

Repeats

Repeats are essentially multiple tempo runs combined into an interval training format. The key differences between repeats and intervals lie in the recovery time and the interval pace. Repeats utilize long rest periods during which the runner is allowed to recover fully before doing another fast run. The rest periods often use walking for the intermediate activity. The fast run pace for repeats is usually a function of race pace or race pace goal rather than aerobic potential as are the interval workouts. Terms often used to describe repeat paces are "date pace", about 90% of the runners current race pace capability and "goal pace", the runners goal race pace. Repeats are very useful to runners with good mileage bases training for shorter races. This technique allows them to run multiple runs of up to 1/4 of their race distance in a single workout (i.e. repeated miles or mile an one halfs for a 10K workout). Beginners should start with less distance and fewer repeats run at or below 90% of their current race pace ability. They can then build up to a maximum of total repeat run mileage equal to around 10% of their weekly mileage base and speed of near their goal pace.

Fartlek

Fartlek is an unstructured form of speedwork often done on varied or cross country terrain. During a moderately paced run, the runner varies his speed by periodically accelerating to harder paces and then slowing back down to the moderate pace. The object is to maintain an average level of effort of about 90% of race pace. The surges push the effort to near maximum aerobic effort and the slower paces are a 75-80% effort for recovery. Fartlek is a very effective simulation of passing and surging in shorter races and is useful in building aerobic power and speed especially when done on hilly terrain. It provides a pleasant alternative to structured track interval workouts and provides the extra benefits of running hills and utilizing different muscle groups.

Race Specific Training

During the sharpening phase of training, it is important to consider the specifics of the particular race for which you are training. Your training runs should be tailored to simulate as closely as possible the terrain, the surface and environment in which you expect to race.

Sharpening Programs

The following are examples of several programs which can be used to develop a schedule for the sharpening phase of marathon training.

Beginning Marathon Sharpening

Prerequisites: Base of 40 miles per week including a long run of between 15 and 20 miles.

Goals: To build marathon endurance by completing four 20 mile training runs. To develop marathon pace through short tempo runs.

Mileage Progression

Week	S	M	T	W	T	F	S	Total
18	16	2	4	2T	4	8	0	40
19	20	2	4	8	4	8	0	46
20	16	2	4	2T	4	8	0	40
21	20	2	4	8	4	8	0	46
22	16	2	4	2T	4	8	0	40
23	20	2	4	8	4	8	0	46
24	20	2	4	2T	4	8	0	44
25	16	2	4	8	4	8	0	42

(T) Tempo runs consist of 2 mile warmup, the indicated number of miles at marathon race pace and a 2 mile jog to cool down.

Total includes warm up and cool down miles for tempo runs.

All runs are done at an easy pace (75-80% effort).

Intermediate Marathon Sharpening

Prerequisites: Base of 60 miles per week including a long run of 20 miles.

Goals: To establish a strong endurance base by completing 6-8 runs of 20 miles or more. To develop marathon pace and aerobic potential through a program of tempo runs.

Mileage Progression

Week	S	M	T	W	T	F	S	Total
18	20	6	6	3T	6	12	6	61
19	20	6	6	4T	6	12	6	62
20	18-20	6	6	4T	6	12	6	60-62
21	20	6	6	5T	6	12	6	63
22	18-20	6	6	5T	6	12	6	61-63
23	20	6	6	6T	6	12	6	64
24	20	6	6	6T	6	12	6	64
25	20	6	6	6T	6	12	6	64

(T) Tempo runs consist of one mile warmup at easy pace, the indicated mileage at marathon race goal pace, and a one or more mile jog to cool down.

Total includes warmup and cool down miles for tempo runs.

All other runs are at an easy pace (75-80% effort).

Advanced Marathon Sharpening

Prerequisite: Base of 75 miles per week including a long run of 25 miles and previous speedwork at marathon race pace or faster.

Goals: To establish strong endurance base by completing 8 long runs of between 20 and 30 miles. To peak marathon potential with specific speedwork.

Mileage Progression

Week	S	M	T	W	T	F	S	Total
18	25	7	7	5T	7	14	7	68-74
19	25	7	7	5T	7	14*	7	68-74
20	25	7	7	6T	7	14*	7	69-75
21	25	7	7	6T	7	14*	7	69-75
22	25	7	7	6T	7	14*	7	69-75
23	25	7	7	7T	7	14*	7	69-75
24	25	7	7	7T	7	14*	7	69-75
25	25	7	7	7T	7	14	7	69-75

(T) Tempo runs consist of 1 mile warm up at easy pace, the indicated mileage at marathon goal pace, and a 1 or more mile jog to cool down.

*The Friday run can be optionally a strength run of 6 to 7 miles of hard effort (either intervals, fartlek or hill training) with a 1 mile warm up and a 1 mile or more jog to cool down. (See Appendix for examples). No strength work is done on the final Friday to allow adequate recovery before the race.

Total includes warmup and cool down miles for tempo runs.

All other runs are at an easy pace (75-80% effort).

PSYCHOLOGICAL PREPARATION

Training your mind and your emotions is an important phase of marathon training. It can help to align you with the laws of nature. This leads to training with ease, improving with certainty and attaining your true potential.

Earlier, we indicated that one of the psychological attributes to excellence is commitment. The other key is self-control. These keys are unanimous choices of some of the best athletes, coaches and scouts even though they could not agree on the necessary physical attributes. Self-control can be important in being able to perform well under a variety of stress-producing circumstances. Some aspects include being able to accept criticism, not being afraid to fail, maintaining composure under stress and being able to perform to potential during competition. To do these, you need to be able to control and channel your emotions, focus your concentration and bounce back from setbacks.

Behavioral and Rational Strategies

Goal setting is a behavioral approach to self-control which utilizes setting specific goals and self-reinforcement through their achievement. The achieved goal acts as reinforcement and as a stimulus to pursue the next goal, helping to maintain motivation and build self-confidence. Other extrinsic (real) rewards may also help to keep you focused towards achieving a long term goal.

Sometimes the key to solving problems is the ability to view things in a rational and constructive manner. One way to do this is to prevent anxiety from arising. Anxiety arises mainly from irrational or illogical beliefs. Some of these beliefs are that you must always have the approval of those you love; that you must do everything extremely well; that you cannot control or change your feelings; or that you must worry about something that seems fearsome or dangerous. The way to reduce unwanted and unproductive anxiety is to challenge and change some of your irrational beliefs and feelings.

Begin change by questioning the thoughts that upset you. Use self-talk to tell yourself new things. Mental imagery can be used to imagine yourself thinking new thoughts and taking differing courses of action in tough situations. Attempt, in your mind, to see yourself thinking, believing and acting in more constructive ways, then try to duplicate this in real life. If a change in perspective or belief is experienced, try to be aware of what you did or said to make it happen and use that pattern again. Sometimes re-labelling or re-interpreting sensations can put you in control. That knot in your stomach before the race could let you say "I'm so nervous. I hope I don't blow it" or it could signal that your body is saying " I'm pumped up and ready for action. Let's go!" Thoughts control emotions. Become aware of your thoughts and use them to your advantage.

Simulation

Simulation uses practice of desired performance responses and coping strategies in situations as real as you can make them. For the runner, this means that selected competitive situations are reproduced as closely as possible during practice. Introduce yourself to the expected things. Run the race course; run in all kinds of expected weather conditions; practice drinking fluids at specific intervals; run when hungry, after eating, during the expected time of the race (morning, afternoon, etc.), or when you are tired. Then introduce the unexpected - practice passing people, having others pass you, have your friends come out during your run and say "Looking good" or whatever bothers you.

Human modeling is another form of simulation which attempts to emulate, model or reproduce the positive behavior of another, perhaps highly skilled athlete. Modeling can place you in the position to look at and draw upon other peoples' strengths in order to better your own physical and psychological strengths. For example, watch a video of the Olympic marathons and pretend you're Joan Benoit or Carlos Lopes and imagine yourself running the marathon as they did.

Mental imagery is a form of simulation that takes place in your head. It gives you a chance to deal with an event or problem internally before you must deal with it in real life. For mental imagery to work, you must be able to vividly imagine yourself executing the skill or response. Movement is an important part of mental rehearsal. The moving mental image is felt to allow you to respond to the changes and do the movement needed to execute the action. Imagine yourself running across the finish line at the marathon, look up at the clock - you've done it and in the goal time! Imagery or visualization can be learned by practice. Start with simple familiar scenes and work up. You can watch someone running and try to replay it in your mind. When you are running and are feeling that relaxed, floating, "I could run forever" feeling, try to focus on your mental picture of that effort. Practice seeing that image when you are not running and when you are tired during a run. Use that mental picture to improve the way you feel while you're running. Run the race course, then visualize yourself running it during the race. See yourself taking aid, passing the 20 mile mark running smoothly and relaxed. Picture yourself finishing, the applause and cheers from the spectators, the cold drink you will reward yourself with. You can later use this mental imagery to pinpoint a problem or focus on an area of improvement such as staying relaxed during the last 6 miles.

Relaxation

Sometimes you are too tense or too anxious to achieve your best performance. Having the ability to physically relax and calm yourself mentally allows you to reach an optimum level of activation to enhance performance. We all have the body responses to the onset of stress - muscle tenseness, queasy stomach, increased heart rate, etc. Become aware of your body signals and use them as your signals to relax. You can focus on relaxing different muscles in your body. You can use deep breathing. Follow each breath with an effort to relax or use mental imagery to imagine yourself in a relaxed state. There are several relaxation procedures you can learn including progressive relaxation, but all need frequent practice. Relaxation may help you to get a good night sleep before the race as well as during the race.

The most important relaxation tool to learn is deep or diaphragmatic breathing which can give an immediate sense of relaxation throughout the body while you are running. This type of breathing also allows more oxygen to be taken in and get into the blood leading to better physical and mental performance. Diaphragmatic or belly breathing works by the expansion of the lower abdomen creating a vacuum in the chest which causes air to be drawn into the lower lungs. As the middle lungs fill, the upper abdomen expands and finally the chest expands as the upper lungs are filled. To practice, lie on your back with your hands on your abdomen just above your navel. Exhale completely. Inhale through your nose allowing your abdomen to expand. As you fill your lungs completely, exhale through your mouth. Practice by blowing all your air out through your mouth using your abdominal muscles and pushing down with your hands. Then inhale again through your nose filling your lungs completely and exhale by blowing the air out through your mouth. Practice about 5 complete cycles. Note the relaxed feeling throughout your body. This type of breathing is useful while you are running. Concentrate on belly breathing inhaling through both nose and mouth when you begin to feel tired or when you are running uphill. The increased oxygen and relaxed upper body should make the running seem easier.

Focus

Concentration involves changing the focus of attention during the event. Focus is awareness of one thing to the exclusion of others. It must be adjustable from narrow (my calf feels tight) to broad (how hard am I working to run this pace). It is important to learn when each of these is necessary. An interplay of relaxation and focus then becomes a concentration cycle, such as, from the mind (seeing yourself running relaxed), to body (relaxing the calf muscle) to target (centering on running this mile).

Sometimes learning to shift attention is important to learn to change the focus. Let your mind run free, then bring it back to the necessary focus and repeat the cycle.

If you are interested in learning more about sports psychology, read either *Peak Performance* by Charles A. Garfield or *The Warrior Athlete* by Dan Millman. Both will give you specific techniques and exercises to help you improve your performance from a psychological focus. Both are excellent, but have slightly different emphasis with *The Warrior Athlete* being more esoteric.

PEAKING

Peaking is the ability to optimize your performance for a particular race or race series. It is both a long and short term mental and physical focus on a goal.

Long term focus involves goal setting 6 or more months in advance and devising a long term training plan. For the marathon, this usually involves a 4 to 6 month stamina and endurance building phase with little or no speed work (base building), followed by a 2 month specific endurance speed, terrain and environment training phase (sharpening), followed by a short rest and loading phase (tapering) during the week preceding the event. By devising the long term plan and goals, mental focus is put on the marathon from the outset and training is directed at that goal.

Short term focus begins during the sharpening phase. During this phase, training is directed towards topping off aerobic fitness and simulating race conditions. Marathon specific speed work is utilized, heat acclimatization may be performed and familiarity with the marathon terrain is acquired. During this period, training mileage is not increased but rather it should be reduced when speed work is added. Specificity and, for advanced runners, intensity will be increased. The desired effect is to reach maximal marathon readiness the day of the race, not one week early nor one week late.

Psychological Peaking

The basis for psychological peaking is goal setting, goal achievement and reinforcement throughout the training period. By reaching each goal, intermediate as well as ultimate, along the way to the marathon, you become certain that you are prepared and ready to race when race day arrives. Marathon performances do not happen accidentally, they are designed and built.

Throughout your training period, it is important to

visualize what you plan to do in the race. Use your feelings and senses during training to learn how you might feel during the marathon so that you will be prepared for the various phases of the race. Learn to listen to and monitor your body so that you will understand what it is saying.

In the sharpening phase of your program, when the training is highly specific, you should have excellent simulation of the race. This can be enhanced even further running on similar terrain, at the same time of day and even on the marathon course itself. Familiarize yourself with the course so that you can run through the race many times in your mind. Concentrate on the following items while you are doing your training runs:

- **Self Assessment** : learn to know your own body and its responses during training runs. Practice new tactics, eating habits such as carbo loading, and drinking water while on training runs. Learn what motivates you. Use your training diary to learn what factors are associated with best and worst runs (ie. thinking, focus, what you've eaten, how much rest or sleep you've gotten, etc.). Use your own patterns to your best advantage.

- **Listen to your body** : learn to monitor your body signals while you are running. Do body scans or body checks such as "how do my feet feel, are my calf muscles relaxed, is my breathing regular and not too fast, is my upper body tense, are my jaws and teeth clenched".

- **Talk to your body** : pick some key words that work for you such as relax, smooth, float or whatever and practice saying and responding to them. Do a body scan and repeat your key word 5-10 times in a row while exhaling.

- **Relax** : use relaxation techniques to get a good night's sleep, to remain calm, run smoothly and conserve energy during your long runs.

- **Imagery** : use imagery during training to see yourself overcoming obstacles and to feel yourself running comfortably (smooth, relaxed and in control). Use images of smoothly running animals, relaxed settings or powerful machinery to get body responses. Intersperse verbal reminders to drink fluids, maintain pace and focus on form.

- **Learning to deal with discomfort** : an adequate training program combined with proper race pacing should prevent intense pain during the marathon. However, pain does sometimes occur. Note the normal sensations of fatigue during your long training runs so that you will know what to expect during the race. Most of what is felt in the marathon is discomfort due to fatigue or simply the sane body talking to the insane master "What are you doing to me, I'm tired". The master can answer "I'm the master here and I want to finish, it's not much farther, We can do it!".

- **Simulation** : practice on the actual course, learn the best way to divide it into sections. Practice body scan, self talk and other psychological tools. Use your imagination to see yourself running as a graceful animal, imagine a giant hand pushing you uphill. Run when tired and practice dealing with discomfort. Think of any problems that might arise and figure out how to simulate them and cope with them. Practice racing and running your own pace during that race. Practice passing others or having them pass you. The best way to convince yourself that you can do something is to do it. Keep working on the long training runs until you know you can run for the length of time the marathon will take.

RACE PREPARATION

RACE PREPARATION

Tapering

The final phase of training is tapering or resting prior to the event. Each runner responds to tapering approaches differently and many personalized schemes are used. The following physiological principles apply, however, and should be considered when selecting a tapering method.

- Rebuilding depleted nutrient stores in the body (such as glycogen) to their maximum requires 2 to 3 days of lowered activity.

- Rebuilding minor injuries in muscle or connective tissue takes a minimum of 5 days.

- The body's store of oxidative enzymes diminishes in 72 hours if not stimulated by aerobic exercise.

- Any training effect from hard activity during the last 10 days before the race will be minimal.

You should back off before the event, but not totally stop running. One recommended approach to marathon tapering is given below. Begin the week before race week. During this week the final sharpening and the last hard workouts will be done. No long run should be done the weekend before the race, instead an easy run of less distance, 10 to 15 miles, should be run. Four days before the race a normal length easy workout is run possibly incorporating a few accelerations (essentially an easy fartlek (EF) run), to loosen up the legs. The next two days easy workouts of about half the normal length should be run. The day before the marathon an easy run of about 15 minutes is useful in keeping the legs loose and for burning off excess nervous energy.

Carbohydrate loading is an important part of this pattern with the last three days before the marathon the time for the runner to increase carbohydrate intake while avoiding fats and protein. Typical tapering schemes are shown below. The last week of sharpening is shown for comparison.

Beginning Marathon Tapering

Goals: Last long run 2 weeks before to allow complete recovery. Mileage cut to less than half during the last 4 days for rest and carbohydrate loading.

Week	S	M	T	W	T	F	S	Total
25	16	2	4	8	4	8	0	42
26	10	2	4	4	2*	2*	jog*	25
27 Race								

The jog is a short one done at a very easy pace for 10-15 minutes. All other runs are done at and easy pace (75-80% effort).

*Carbohydrate Load

Intermediate Marathon Tapering

Goals: Last long run 2 weeks before to allow complete recovery. Mileage cut to less than half during last 4 days for rest and carbohydrate loading. Some short accelerations in workout 4 days before marathon to keep legs loose.

Week	S	M	T	W	T	F	S	Total
25	20	6	6	6T	6	12	6	62
26	12	6	6	6EF	3*	3*	jog*	38
27	Race							

The jog is a short one done at an easy pace for about 15 minutes.

The short EF (easy fartlek) run is an easy paced run (75-80% effort) with 6-8 marathon race pace striding sessions of around 200 yards interspersed throughout.

All other tapering week runs done at an easy pace (75-80% effort).

*Carbohydrate load

Advanced Marathon Tapering

Goals: Last long run 2 weeks before to allow complete recovery. Mileage cut to less than half during last 4 days for rest and carbohydrate loading. Some short accelerations in workout 4 days before marathon to keep legs loose.

Week	S	M	T	W	T	F	S	Total
25	25	7	7	7T	7	14	7	69
26	15	7	7	7EF	3*	3*	jog*	44
27	Race							

The jog is a short one done at an easy pace for about 15 minutes.

The short EF (easy fartlek) run is an easy paced run (75-80% effort) with 6-8 marathon race pace striding sessions of around 200 yards interspersed throughout.

All other tapering week runs done at an easy pace (75-80% effort).

*Carbohydrate load

Carbohydrate loading

Previously, you have read about the major sources of energy and have, hopefully, used them in running. We hope your training experience has permitted you to run faster using fat metabolism and to store more carbohydrates (CHO) or glycogen to be used. You also remember that some glycogen metabolism must be happening for fat metabolism to easily occur. It is possible to store even more carbohydrates through a process called carbohydrate loading. Normal stores of carbohydrates will last for 1-1/2 to 2 hours of running, but CHO loading can be a useful tool for events that last longer than this, such as the marathon.

Carbohydrate loading has been studied intensely by many exercise physiologists. The original plan involved a six day program with a 3 day depletion phase to trigger supercompensation by the muscles causing them to store more glycogen. David Costill's Ball State Human Performance Lab has done extensive studies that show an intensely training endurance athlete depletes his muscles to low levels daily and therefore does not need dietary induction of the depletion phase. This athlete normally needs a high CHO diet to replenish his/her muscle stores. Costill's studies showed that eating a high CHO diet (70%) following a normal 50% CHO diet leads to almost the same muscle glycogen stores as 70% CHO following 15% CHO (depletion phase). The high CHO diet must be accompanied by a reduction in exercise for this to occur. This information leads us to the following recommended loading scheme.

Marathon Week

M	T	W	T	F	S	S
Regular Exercise Regular Diet (50-60% CHO)			Low Exercise High Carbohydrate Diet (70-80% CHO)			RACE

Costill's research has also revealed that for more than a 48 hour loading phase, complex carbo's produce greater muscle glycogen storage than do simple carbohydrates. The daily requirements for protein and fat should be fulfilled; but the more carbohydrates that are eaten, the more will be stored. Glycogen storage is facilitated by two large meals rather than smaller ones. Our recommended plan is:

- Carbohydrate load for 3 days before the event; accompany this with a period of reduced exercise level.

- The first day of loading is the most important. Begin with a big carbo breakfast, such as pancakes or French toast. This is the day for the traditional pasta dinner of spaghetti and bread. Try to stuff in as many complex carbohydrates as possible in these two meals.

- Taper off bulky complex carbohydrates and switch to more simple CHO's as the race approaches. Do not load on large quantities of fruit or any other foodstuffs that you don't normally eat. These may cause intestinal upset or diarrhea.

- The last major meal should be 12-15 hours before the race, should not include too much bulk and should be easily digestible so that it will pass through your system before the race. Experiment with this meal before your long training runs so that you know what and how much of the desired food works best for you. We have found 1 or 2 bean burritos with very little cheese works well for us. We always take our own pre-race dinner with us after having bad experiences from eating untried food in strange restaurants.

- If you plan to eat on race day morning and are used to doing so, a light CHO meal such as toast may be consumed 2-3 hours before the race. This meal is certainly a matter of personal preference and should be done only if this is usual for you. No carbo's, especially simple sugars, should be ingested within 2 hours of the run; this could lead to an blood insulin reaction causing weakness and fatigue.

How will you know if you are effectively loading? If you are keeping a record of your daily weight, you will notice a 2-5 or more pound weight gain over the 3 day period. As the CHO is stored, water is also stored in the muscle leading to the weight gain. This water storage may make your legs feel sluggish during your few miles of easy runs, but it may well come in handy during the marathon as a source of sweat and cooling. You may also feel sleepy, cranky or tired due to the blood sugar and insulin responses to all the carbohydrate. During the race however, you should feel superpowered and ready to go.

Carbohydrate loading without the depletion phase should be safe for most healthy individuals. Diabetics and others with any health problems should consult a physician before any radical diet changes.

PLANNING YOUR RACE

The biggest problem may be to decide whether you should run. You may feel unprepared, have an injury, have an illness or other similar problems. You, of course, must make the decision. Even though not running may be a major disappointment, remember that there are other marathons, your training will last for a while and you can easily continue to build on what you've already achieved. One race is never worth a major permanent injury. If you feel unprepared, you can run slower than you planned or run just part of the race.

Strategies and Tactics

Long before you toe the starting line, you should have an overall strategy for the race. As a minimum, your finish goal, time splits, the number of aid stops and type of aid you will take should be planned in advance. Contingency plans for adverse weather and other conditions also should be considered. Once you have established the race plan, the race itself should be reduced to a series of bite sized goals leading to your finish goal.

Setting a Reasonable Finish Time Goal

In a marathon, there are two things which determine how fast you can run: your aerobic potential and your endurance. Your aerobic potential can be determined from your performances at shorter races and extrapolated to give you a reasonably accurate idea of your marathon potential. One simple way to do this is to take a current 10K race time and multiply by 4.7 to get an estimate of your potential marathon time. A 40 minute 10K performance would lead to a 3:08 marathon while a 50 minute 10K predicts a 3:55 marathon. The training pace charts in the appendix give goal times and paces based on various 10K times. The time you get will be a reasonable estimate of the best time you could run for a marathon given your current aerobic fitness.

Now the bad news, unless you are an experienced

marathoner with adequate endurance training, you will find it difficult to run a marathon at your potential. This is because a marathon has specific physical and mental endurance requirements that are only obtained through proper training and experience. (See the previous sections on specificity and endurance training).

Without these, you can expect a degradation of 10-20% from the best time estimate given above. If you feel that you don't have enough endurance training or you have never run a marathon, set your finish time goal 10% or so slower than the best time estimate. It is much more enjoyable to finish strongly than to experience the sensations people have variously described as "hitting the wall", "being jumped by a bear", "crashing" or "dying". The beginner's first and foremost goal should be to finish!

Splits

To provide subgoals, and to monitor your progress along the race course, you should compute a series of intermediate times or "splits" and memorize them or write them down on something that can be carried along.

Although it is generally accepted that more even splits (constant pace) provide the best results, some runners prefer to use negative (start slow, finish fast) or positive (start fast, finish slow) techniques.

Those using negative splits usually describe races where the technique has been effective as being very positive psychologically because they feel stronger than everyone else at the end. It is a major boost to pass people during the last few miles. For some runners this self reinforcement may aid performance enough to compensate for the slow start.

Positive splits ("money in the bank" or "kamikaze" approaches) are used as a strategy by some competitive runners to force the pace of their opponents. Running much faster than your average pace at the beginning of a long distance event will almost certainly result in early glycogen depletion and unpleasant feelings. Because some seasoned runners are very good at dealing with these feelings, they can use this as a winning strategy. However, positive splits are seldom used by knowledgeable runners as a strategy for running the best time. They must be *avoided* at all costs *by beginners*. Pace training is a great aid to this.

Write down your splits and carry them with you. The difficulty of performing high level math in your head while running in a race is well established. Splits can be written on wristbands, upside down on your race number or on various parts of your body with indelible ink. (Make certain that the ink or paper used is sweat and water proof).

The splits recommended here are for even effort. On a flat marathon course, you can calculate your average pace per mile by dividing your finish goal time by 26.22. By multiplying the pace per mile by the distance, you can determine target split times for different distances along the course. You should figure out, at least, each of the first 3 miles and the 5, 10, 15 and 20 mile splits. This will allow you to confirm proper pace early and then to check your progress along the way. If you have trouble maintaining a specific pace, you may want to check your splits every mile. If the course has hills, you should not maintain a constant pace. Your splits should allow for even effort which is slowing down on uphill and speeding up on downhill sections. A good rule of thumb for uphill of 100 feet/mile gain is to add 20 to 30 seconds/mile to your average pace while on steep uphill of 200 ft/mi add 40 to 70 seconds/mile. For downhill, subtract 15 to 20 seconds/mile for 100 ft/mi and 20 to 40 seconds for 200 ft/mi.

Course Knowledge

Many races have been won and lost because of course knowledge. These include examples as catastrophic as getting lost and as simple as having the inside position on the last turn before the finish. The last thing you want during a race is a surprise. Even good surprises have negative consequences and may leave you wondering if you could have done better if you had only known....

Knowledge of a race course can be divided into 3 pieces, the start, the main body of the course and the finish. Knowledge of the body of the course can be obtained in the weeks prior to the race by studying maps, topographical drawings, pictures, films and talking with others who have been on the course or better yet, by going over the course yourself by car, bicycle or on several early training runs. The important things to determine are the location and degree of any obstacles such as hills, tight turns or constricted areas and the location of dominant landmarks such as turn around points, aid stations, and points where you might want split times. Other items to consider are the type of surface you will be running on and exposure to potential winds, sun, rain etc. If you can, check out the course at the same time of day as the race will occur.

Little knowledge of the start and finish areas can be obtained prior to race day. If possible these areas should be viewed before the race for their general features and terrain. Knowledge of the finish may mean the difference between winning and losing precious seconds toward a personal or age group record. You should know *exactly* where the finish is and exactly when you could start to sprint if you wanted to. Notice if there is a turn or corner just before the finish and how far it is from this to the line. If there are turns near the finish, determine the best position to be in going through them (i.e. the route giving the shortest distance to the finish).

Other Plans

A planned race has the best chance of being a successful race. Your goal for the race should be determined in advance, with the training phase physically and psychologically geared for successful accomplishment of the goal. Last minute changes usually lead to disaster.

Planing the race includes knowing other aspects such as:

- How long it takes to get from your house or hotel to the race and how long it takes to find a parking place (or both).

- The locations of the bathrooms at the start and along the course.

- The place to leave and retrieve your warmups.

- The location of aid stations and the types of aid available.

- The place to meet your family or friends.

We have included a checklist of items you should need on race day. Use this and add anything else you might need. Plan your clothing needs by keeping weather differences in mind. The shoes you are going to wear should not be brand new, but should have been worn several times and be comfortable. Prepare, lay out or pack these items from a list ahead of time so you can just walk out the door for the race and know that you are prepared.

Equipment Checklist for the Marathon

- _____ Shoes
- _____ Insoles
- _____ Orthotics
- _____ Socks
- _____ Shorts
- _____ Singlet
- _____ Underwear
- _____ Watch
- _____ Short sleeved T shirt
- _____ Long sleeved T shirt
- _____ Running tights
- _____ Jacket and Pants (either wind or warm up)
- _____ Hat, sweatband or kerchief
- _____ Gloves or mittens
- _____ Change of clothes for afterwards
- _____ Extra shoelaces
- _____ Number if picked up early
- _____ Safety pins
- _____ Course Map
- _____ Race Instructions
- _____ Splits
- _____ Felt tip or ballpoint pen
- _____ Paper tape, bandaids
- _____ Athletic tape
- _____ Vaseline
- _____ Powder
- _____ Deodorant
- _____ Sunscreen
- _____ Towel
- _____ Prerace food and fluids
- _____ Postrace food and fluids
- _____ Money

Rest and Adaptation

Adequate rest and sleep is extra important in the tapering phase. The most important night's sleep seems to be two nights before the race. Plan your week's schedule accordingly. If you are sleepless the night before the race, don't worry, so are most others. Many records have been set with little or no sleep the night before.

If you are traveling to the race, we suggest that you arrive early in the day preceding it. Review the course if possible. We have found that arriving several days to a week ahead in a different time zone or environment throws you completely off schedule without allowing adequate time to adjust. Arriving the day before seems to be extremely important if traveling to either high altitude or a hot climate. Best performances without adaptation at altitude are within 24-48 hours of arrival. Some short term adaptation takes place in the first 24 hours, but performance declines are noted in the period between 2 days and 1 month after arrival. Arriving several days early in a hot climate may dehydrate you before the race.

RACING

RACING

"NO NEW IS GOOD NEW" Race time is the time for tried methods, foods, shoes, and equipment. *Never* try anything for the first time in a race.

Race Morning

Set your alarm to wake up early so you have plenty of time before the race. You need to be awake and alert. It is also important to get your body functioning and have a bowel movement to get rid of last night's final carbohydrates. Sometimes drinking 1-2 cups of water or coffee will assist in this process.

Eating on race day was covered in the carbohydrate loading section. If the race is in the late morning or early afternoon, consider a light carbohydrate breakfast of toast with little or no butter.

Getting ready

Your final plans for clothes and shoes will actually depend on the weather. Remember that you will probably be running faster than in training runs; dress accordingly. Too many or too few clothes may be detrimental to performance. The ideal condition is to feel slightly chilly when lined up for the start. Wearing layers that can be removed may be appropriate.

Your race number must always be worn on the front. You may want to fold it or cut it to fit on your shorts so you can take off shirt layers if necessary. If there is a removable tag, be sure it is free.

The choice between training and racing shoes for the marathon is certainly up to the individual. If you're experienced and race often, you may feel racing shoes give you an added edge. If you're not used to racing flats, their lack of cushioning and/or support over 26 miles may not compensate for the few ounces of reduced weight. To prevent the infamous "black toe" and other foot problems, shoes should have at least a thumb's width of length beyond your longest toe when standing.

Preventing chafing over the marathon distance is important. Vaseline or other athletic skin lubricant can be put wherever 2 body surfaces will rub together or where the edge or seam on clothing will rub on the skin. Paper tape over nipples is a good idea especially for men or when running in the rain. Women should wear the same type of bra worn in training. Powder in the shoes or vaseline on the feet can reduce blisters and hot spots. Remember to experiment with any of these ideas on training runs well before the race.

Pick up gear assembled from the checklist and leave for the race giving yourself enough time to park, check on details, warm up and get ready to run.

Before the Start

After arriving, note:

- The location of the bathrooms. Nervousness may lead to several visits. Get in line early, there's usually a crowd.

- Where to put and retrieve your warmups.

- Where to meet your companions.

- The location of the finish area, if it is adjacent to the start. Try to get some knowledge of the finish chute system. Some races use different chutes for different ages and sexes. Find out which chute you must use and exactly where the line is relative to the chute, banners or other landmarks.

Warming Up

Warming up before the event has both psychological and physiological benefits. Physiologically, the increased blood flow and muscle core temperature can be beneficial as can the facilitation and recruitment of the motor units. Warming up may help you to prevent injury during the run by having your body prepared and ready to go. Psychologically, it may help you to become clearly focused on the event and on your body. It may burn off a little of the pre-race "hype" and allow you to run the first mile at or near the desired split time. Often being in the crowd and being primed and ready to go can make you go crazy the first mile and run 30 seconds to a minute per mile faster than you wanted. This burns off glycogen which will be needed later. Be warned that warming up might also make it easy to run the first mile too fast because you are loose. Establishing a routine of pre-race activities which become "automatic" can also help calm you.

Use a walk to slow jog to warm up the muscles and the core temperature slowly without causing fatigue or reducing energy stores. Start jogging about 20 minutes before the race starts. Slowly run for 5 to 10 minutes, then carefully do some easy stretching. Do not stretch before the race unless you have warmed up the muscles because a muscle pull or strain at this time would be catastrophic. After stretching, you may want to do a little bit of striding at race pace before getting into the start staging area. Warm up in your warm up clothing and slowly peel down as you get warmer. Warming up should also give you an idea of the amount of clothing necessary for the run. If the temperature is moderate to cool, you should feel chilly while standing in the staging area. If you are comfortable, you either are wearing too many clothes or will need to deal with hot weather running. Relax the last 5 minutes in your starting location.

Starting

Your start should be planned to provide the shortest, most obstacle free route to the first turn, if there is one. Start toward the side of the road in the direction of the first turn. If the course narrows appreciably after the start, by design or due to parked vehicles, you may want to start more toward the middle of the road. Find out whether runners are to be seeded by pace and, if so, position yourself toward the front of your pace group at the start. If there is no seeding system, get far enough forward in the pack to be near runners of your ability. You can usually tell by their appearance. When in doubt, ask people around you how fast they plan to run. Avoid positioning yourself near runners of vastly different abilities. This usually results in a certain amount of jostling at the start and the potential of someone falling and getting trampled.

While waiting for the gun, you may want to use relaxation techniques to stay calm. It is extremely important not to get too nervous and lose control at the start.

When the gun goes off, start concentrating on the task at hand. Relax, find a clear spot in which to run and establish your pre-planned race pace. It is very easy to run too fast at the start. If you feel like you are running smoothly at an easy training pace, your speed is probably just right!

The First Ten Miles

If you have trained adequately and are healthy, the first 5 to 10 miles should seem very easy to you. Many runners pass this time socializing with others. During this period of the race you want to establish a rhythm of pace, taking aid and meeting intermediate goals. Use concentration cycles to monitor these items and your various body sensations. Lock yourself into a smooth relaxed stride.

The Second Ten Miles

Somewhere in the second ten miles, runners start to get more serious about the marathon. Socializing will abate some as inner concentration cycles become more important. This is the time the physical and mental simulation you practiced before the race pay off as you pass goal after goal just as if you've done it all before. Use self-talk to maintain your concentration.

The Last Six Miles

This is by far the most demanding part of the marathon. If you have prepared adequately and followed your race plan, you should have no difficulty. You will feel fatigue, muscle tightness and soreness during this stage. You may also go through psychological highs and lows. None of these things should surprise you. You have experienced similar feelings on your long training runs and know that they are normal. Encourage yourself with self-talk. Imagery can be used to advantage during this stage to maintain and even lengthen your stride. Picture yourself running as smoothly and effortlessly as you were running at the start of the race.

Somewhere during the last six miles, you will realize that you are going to finish! This usually gives you a big lift. Use it to help you. Start thinking of all the rewards at the finish line and how you will enjoy yourself after the race. Start congratulating yourself, you deserve it! But, don't lose concentration on the goal.

Finishing

Make sure you run all the way through the finish line at the end of the race. Run until someone stops you or gives you a T shirt. Try to keep walking through the chute, stopping immediately drops blood pressure and gives rise to nausea. Try to stay in finish order and keep the other runners in order, this helps the race director give correct times and places to the runners.

If you can, do some kind of cool down, either an easy jog or a walk of 10 minutes or so to allow your blood pressure to return to normal and your muscles to cool down. Do not stop abruptly or sit or lay down. This may lead to a rapid drop in blood pressure, possible fainting, leg cramps, and/or nausea. Do not stretch. Stretching exhausted muscles is a sure way to injure them. A massage, if one is available, feels great and helps to relax the legs. Ice any areas that are sore by massaging them for about 10 minutes with an ice popsicle or ice cubes.

Avoid getting in hot water for extended periods after the race as it may cause swelling. A hot shower is OK. A long soak in the hot tub may feel good at the time but may result in swelling in the muscles making them feel sore.

Drink fluids, especially ones rich in electrolytes such as orange juice or tomato juice (now is the time for electrolyte drinks vs during the race). You can drink a few beers now using them as a reward and to relax aching muscles. It is also necessary to keep drinking water throughout the rest of the day. Drink at least one glass every 1-2 hours. Eat some food, whatever looks good. A large balanced meal may be the best since it will probably contain some of everything you need to replace.

Other Tips and Tactics

Remarkable as it seems, many runners complete 26.2 miles and miss important standards such as Olympic Trial Qualification by only 1 or 2 seconds. Could they have run faster? Probably. How? By paying attention to small details throughout the race. These are the things that experienced road racers do automatically.

Cutting Corners

First of all, this is not cheating. The only race courses which are "guaranteed" to be accurate are those which are "certified". In this country, courses are certified by the TAC (The Athletics Congress of the AAU) to meet international standards set by the IAAF (International Amateur Athletic Federation). Certification is handled by the NRDC (National Running Data Center) in Tucson Arizona. The NRDC requires that courses be measured over the shortest route open to the runners. This means that the course is measured on a route which cuts all corners as closely as possible to the inside apex, usually within 6 inches of the road edge. *You are cheating yourself if you do not cut the corners as the course was measured.* If you run down the center of the road, each right angle turn will cost you about 1 second in your finish time. To further ensure that courses are not short, the NRDC recommends all courses be set up to be 0.1% long, about 50 yards or 8-16 seconds in a marathon.

To run the shortest route, keep as close as possible to the inside edge of the road on all turns and as you come out of the turn assume a straight line route to the inside of the next turn.

Drafting

Many of the current world records for sprinting events in track and field were set at high altitude. The reason for this is the reduction in wind resistance afforded by the "thinner" air. Unfortunately, long distance aerobic events suffer at high altitude because of the lowered ability of the body to transport oxygen to the working muscles. However, even at sea level, a significant reduction in wind resistance can be achieved by a technique known as drafting. As you move through the air, you create a pocket of air behind you that is traveling at the same speed you are. Anyone behind you who is in this pocket does not have to push any air out of the way since it is already moving at his speed. In tests done on bicyclists, it has been shown that nearly 70% of the energy used at 10 miles/hour is due to wind resistance. Bicycling is much more efficient than running. However, a significant reduction in effort can still be realized by drafting when you run, especially into a headwind (wind resistance goes up with the square of the windspeed).

The pocket of air where drafting is effective forms a wedge trailing off at 45 degrees from a runner's shoulder and is probably effective 1 or 2 yards behind him. This means you have to have to run close to someone, close enough to step on his heels or right on his shoulder and slightly behind him. If you can find 3 or 4 or more runners in a close pack, tuck in behind them for a really good draft.

Be warned that some runners do not like to be drafted especially into headwinds where you are getting an obvious advantage. In this situation, you might best offer to trade off the lead every mile or so with one or more runners so that everyone can benefit.

Taking Aid

Some runners still refuse to stop at aid stations for fear of losing precious seconds. In a marathon, it is absolutely critical that you get enough fluids. Dehydration may cause you to slow significantly in the latter stages of the race or drop out entirely with cramps or sickness. You can get enough fluids at aid stations yet still not lose time if you practice drinking and you drink and use the aid stations efficiently. Some people are good at running with cups of water in their hands, other spill most of it. If you are a spiller, learn how to chug the water down rapidly. Often aid stations are long enough to do this twice while you are passing through them.

Most of the large marathons have aid stations every couple of miles. This means you can get enough fluids without drinking as much at each aid station if you chug some (at least 6 oz) at every station. You will probably drop some, but this will help cool you. If all else fails, stop and walk if that is what is necessary to get an adequate supply of fluids during the run. The short walk may help you to feel better and be ready to go again.

Start drinking fluids at the first aid station. Pick up 1 or more cups at each aid station, pour the extra over your head and shoulders if you need more cooling. Water taken in after the 22 mile point will probably not be used. Stopping at the last few aid stations can sometimes help psychologically. However, if you are having muscle cramps, a slow jog may keep the discomfort at a reasonable level. Stopping to walk may result in more painful cramps.

RECOVERY

RECOVERY

What you do the first few hours and days after a marathon is as important as what you do immediately preceding it. This period is critical to your recovery and your future running. The best aid to recovery is a good training program before the marathon. A training program with a good mileage base leads to faster recovery. If you run the marathon without adequate preparation (in spite of all our suggestions), you will suffer both during and after it. If you train well you can cope with the race and will recover faster.

Recovery Factors

There are a number of factors that are important in recovery. The most important of these are muscle soreness, fatigue and feelings of depression. The recovery period and activities should take these items into account. Some general recommendations will be given. These will be followed by recovery progressions.

Delayed muscle soreness after exercise has been described often. The soreness is a feeling of stiffness and soreness that begins 8 or more hours after exercise and may last 3-4 days.(sometimes a week) Researchers propose several causes:

- Damage to the muscle tissue itself. May be due to depletion of energy reserves or actual degeneration of muscle fibers.

- Accumulation of fluid and breakdown products in the muscle.

- Muscle spasm.

- Overstretching or tears of the connective tissue.

The soreness may be a result of one or more of these causes depending on the individual, his state of training and the activity. The most likely causes after a marathon are depletion of energy reserves and the accumulation of fluid in the muscles.

Pain relief can helped by icing, massage, light activity and slow gentle stretching. All of these things work by increasing the circulation to the area. The increased circulation takes away waste and extra fluid and brings new nutrients. Drinking fluids will help flush the waste products from the body.

Recovery Immediately After The Marathon

A cool down after finishing is important. It may be difficult to do this depending on the finish area. Try an easy jog or a walk of 10 minutes or so. Fainting, leg cramps, and/or nausea may result from stopping suddenly or lying down. Do not stretch now. Your muscle are exhausted and you may activate the stretch reflex leading to cramping or injury. Take advantage of massage if offered. Ask for ice to massage any sore areas. Drink lots of fluids, especially ones rich in electrolytes such as orange juice or tomato juice (now is the time for electrolyte drinks vs during the race). Try to drink at least 6-8 ounces of water every 1-2 hours. Eat something as soon as you can. Many marathons provide "goodie" bags or meals for finishers, take advantage of these. A large balanced meal may be the best since it will probably contain some of everything you need to replace. Avoid long soaks in hot water which may cause swelling and lead to delayed muscle soreness. If you feel like you need a nap, reward yourself with one. Try to take a 10 to 15 minute walk later in the afternoon to keep circulation going.

The Day After the Marathon

Post race depression is quite common. You usually feel a real "high" after finishing especially if you've done well and can talk to other runners and share experiences. The next morning the fatigue and soreness may make you wonder if the marathon was worth it. This letdown is a normal response to meeting your goal and not having a new one. Don't make any plans or predictions until the end of the week. Take time to assess your performance, see if you followed your plan and write down both the good and the bad things that happened. Review your training diary to see what worked well for you and try to pick out any mistakes.

Any exercise you can do will promote circulation and aid healing and recovery. If you feel like you can run, find a flat soft surface to run on such as a track. Start slowly, you may be quite stiff. After running a short distance, your legs should loosen up and running will feel better. This sensation will persist until your muscles start to fatigue and then they will start to stiffen back up. When you feel this begin to happen or if something hurts, you've had enough. When in doubt, don't run any more than you did the day before the marathon (about 10 to 15 minutes). If you feel too sore or stiff to run, take a walk or ride your bike or go swimming for 20 to 30 minutes to get your blood flowing. If anything hurts, ice it after your workout. The long soak in the tub may be OK to take today. Eat anything that looks or sounds good to you. You probably need it and you certainly deserve it. Your whole body will feel fatigued, plan to take it easy and go to bed early.

The Week After the Marathon

You may experience a general lack of energy the following week. The reasons for fatigue are obvious. You have worked hard and deserve to rest. Plan on an early bedtime for at least a week to help you get over the fatigue. Eat well balanced meals with 50-60% complex carbohydrates to replenish the body's energy stores. Take in adequate protein to rebuild any tissue damage. Cravings for particular foods should be answered. This may be the body's way of telling you what it needs.

As the stiffness and soreness subside, slowly build up your runs. Think of it as a sort of reverse tapering process. As you dropped hard workouts, then reduced your mileage down to a minimum the day before the marathon, so should you increase your mileage from a minimum the day after, slowly building it until you are ready to do hard workouts again. The maximum should be the same mileage as the week before the marathon. The minimum should be whatever exercise feels good to you. Several days after the marathon you may feel very strong. This is because your post race lessened activity and eating well have carbohydrate loaded your body! Avoid the temptation to do a hard workout. Unless you are incredibly fit, you have *not* recovered yet. Stick to your recovery plan.

The Month After the Marathon

If you are not an experienced marathoner, expect to have some long term fatigue during the month following the race. This fatigue usually shows up when you try to do hard or long runs. You will simply "run out of gas". It will go away and eventually you will emerge stronger than ever. As a rule of thumb, allow yourself about 10 training miles for every race mile for a full recovery. When you are back doing regular training and have accumulated 260 training miles, you should be ready to race again. Now is the time to set some goals for your future racing and make plans for training.

If you are an experienced marathoner with a good training base, this 260 miles of recovery will happen soon. You are in excellent shape, have peaked and may find that you can run some great races. If you plan to race, cut down on your training mileage and recover fully from each one. If you have not fully recovered from the marathon and try to race, you may run excellent times, but your are courting serious injury. Keep setting goals and planning your training so that you can achieve those goals.

Progressions

Listed below are several post marathon recovery programs. These are only guides. Recovery rates are highly individual and only you can determine whether this program is too short. If soreness or fatigue lingers, back off to the previous week's schedule and give yourself time to heal. If you have persistent pain, you may have injured yourself in the marathon. Try another less stressful aerobic exercise such as bicycling or swimming for awhile. If pain is severe, you may need complete rest and the opinion of a physician.

Beginning Marathon Recovery

Goal: To recover from the marathon and return to desired training program.

Week	S	M	T	W	T	F	S
27	Race	J/W	J/W	J/W	2	4	0
28	4	0	2	4	2	4	0
29	8	0	2	4	2	4	0
30	10	2	2	5	2	5	0

J/W days are short jogs or walks.

All runs done at the an easy pace (75-80% effort) or slower. See easy pace chart in appendix.

Intermediate Marathon Recovery

Goal: To recover from the marathon and return to desired training program.

Week	S	M	T	W	T	F	S
27	Race	J/W	J/W	3	3	6	4
28	10	4	4	8	4	8	4
29	12	4	4	10	4	8	4
30	16	5	5	10	5	10	5

J/W days are short jogs or walks.

All runs done at the an easy pace (75-80% effort) or slower. See easy pace chart in appendix.

Advanced Marathon Recovery

Goal: To recover from the marathon and return to desired training program.

Week	S	M	T	W	T	F	S
27	Race	J/W	3	3	5	9	5
28	15	6	6	12	6	12	6
29	20	7	7	14	7	14	7
30	20+	7	7	14*	7	14	7

J/W day is a short jog or walk.

* This run optionally can be speed work of 6-7 miles. All runs done at the an easy pace (75-80% effort) or slower. See easy pace chart in appendix.

AIDS TO PERFORMANCE

SUPPLEMENTAL TRAINING

The successful runner requires whole body fitness. You can use running as the specific training for running which gives cardiovascular fitness and muscular endurance for the legs. It is important to keep the rest of your body in the best possible condition also. Cross training is a way of training using other types of exercise to aid in the aerobic conditioning necessary for running. Supplemental training means adding training techniques to those that are specific to running to develop and maintain the rest of the body and prevent injury. The totally fit person incurs fewer injuries, performs better and more efficiently. The supplemental techniques discussed here will be stretching, abdominal strengthening and circuit weight training. The last two techniques use endurance methods which give muscular endurance as well as muscular strength.

Stretching

Economy is a measure of a successful training program. Economy of running has been found to correlate with running technique. Economic runners showed smaller changes in mechanical energy during running stride and a greater degree of energy transfer between the body parts. This allows the body to use the energy available with less energy consumption by the involved muscles. One of the most important factors in this concept is flexibility. This is because lack of flexibility restricts the range of motion and may limit the extent of energy transfers. We will not discuss biomechanics of running, but hope to impress upon you the need for flexibility.

Muscles contain receptors called spindles and Golgi tendon organs that provide sensory information regarding changes in the length and tension of the muscle. The main function of the spindles is to respond to stretch in a muscle and, through reflex action, initiate a stronger contraction to reduce this stretch. The stretch reflex mainly responds to voluntary movements and maintains uprignt posture. Impulses from the Golgi tendon organs cause reflex relaxation of the muscle and its opposing muscle. When the actual stretch occurs, the spindles resist the stretch. If the stretch is held longer than 6 seconds, the Golgi tendon organs respond allowing the muscle to reflexively relax. This lengthens the muscle and allows it to remain in a stretched position for a long period reducing the possibility of injury due to the stretching.

The purpose of a stretching program is to relax the muscle and work it through the necessary range of motion. Stretching the muscle at the wrong time or in the wrong way can activate the stretch reflex causing the muscle to contract and become tighter rather than relaxed. Thus, we do not suggest stretching before running when the muscles are cold and tight. Stretching at this time has been shown to lead to injury rather than helping to prevent it. Stretching should be done only after the muscle is warmed up. This may be after a 5 to 10 minute walk or slow jog that should be the beginning of your workout. After the workout may be OK, if you've done a cool down session of gentle exercise. The best suggestion is to set aside some time 3 days per week for your supplemental training which should include a warm up, the main exercises (i.e. circuit weight program) and then 10 to 15 minutes of gentle stretching. The stretching can always be done more often than this. Many runners find a gentle stretching and relaxation program helpful before bedtime.

Stretching is done to relax the muscles and connective tissues. The connective tissue needs 20 seconds to relax and the muscles take about 2 minutes to relax, most of the stretching that is done actually is working on the connective tissue. The stretch should be done slowly and carefully to the point of slight pull or slight discomfort. *It should not be painful!* Bouncing and pushing to the point of pain can activate the stretch reflex negating the purpose of stretching and risking injury. Stretching is not a competitive sport. Flexibility differs with the individual. Your goal should be to achieve a good level of flexibility for you, not match anyone else's level.

The stretching program set out here was developed by our friend and physical therapist, Jim Weggenman of Willamette Physical Therapy. Jim has rehabilitated a large number of athletes and runners including Patti. He suggests that these stretches be done to prevent injury and to provide freedom of movement for better performance.

He uses a system called proprioceptive neuromuscular facilitation, more easily called the "hold-relax" method of stretching which involves a contraction of the muscle followed by a relaxation and a stretch. The tightening "fools" the stretch reflex, activating the Golgi tendon organ. This acts to start relaxing the muscle before the actual stretch begins and allows you to stretch the muscle further.

The Stretches

In all of the stretches the contractions are done by tightening the muscle, not actually moving it. The more you run, the stronger and tighter the muscles of the lower back and the entire backs of the legs become. The first three stretches are for these muscles.

- **Lower Back Muscles**

Position : Lie on your back, holding your knees to your chest. Make certain that the tailbone is lifted off the floor.

Contraction : Push out legs against arms, hold for 6 seconds.

Stretch : Relax, then pull legs toward chest and hold for 20 seconds.

- **Hamstring Muscles in Backs of Thighs**

Position : Sit on floor with one knee bent and the other leg straight. The arm on the side with the bent knee is positioned under the knee or on the shin.

Contraction : Pull heel down against floor, hold for 6 seconds.

Stretch : Relax, reach toward toes with arm on straight leg side. Don't worry if you can't reach your toes. Relax and repeat on other leg.

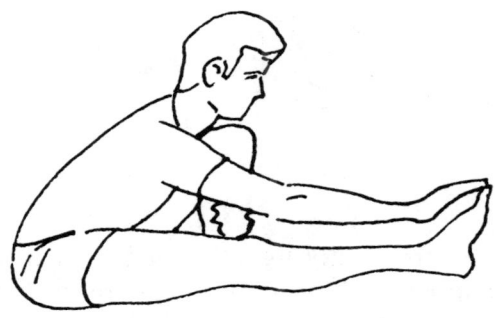

- **Gastrocnemius and Soleus Muscles of the Calves**

Position : Stand leaning against a wall, tree, etc. with one leg bent, the other straight behind you with both heels on the ground.

Contraction : Lean forward with a straight back until stretch is Felt in the calf. Go up on toes for 6 seconds.

Stretch : Come down off toes, relax and lean further forward, hold for 20 seconds. Repeat with back knee bent which stretches the muscles lower down and the Achilles tendon. Repeat with other leg.

Other muscles frequently tight in runners, particulary those doing speed work or hill training are the hip flexors in the fronts of the legs and the adductors in the inside of the thighs.

- **Hip Flexor Muscles**

Position : Kneel on one knee. Position other knee slightly behind or directly over ankle.

Contraction : Try to pull the knee on the floor forward, hold for 6 seconds.

Stretch : Relax, lean forward and hold for 20 seconds.

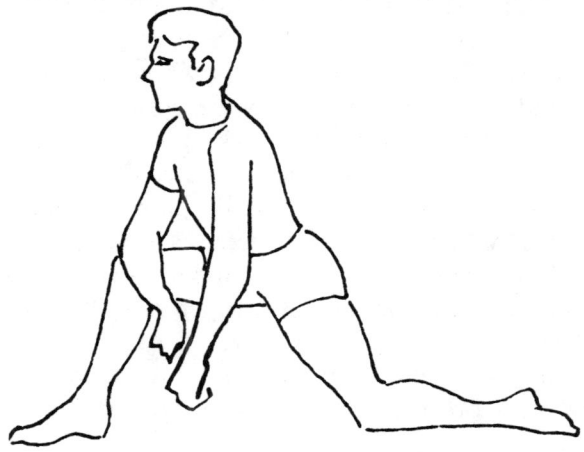

- **Adductors or the Inside Thigh Muscles.**

Position : Sit with the soles of the feet together, hands on knees.

Contraction : Pull knees together against hands, hold for 6 seconds.

Stretch : Relax, let knees fall downward towards the floor, hold for 20 seconds.

Other safe and useful stretches can be found in Judy Alter's *Surviving Exercise*. This book also tells you stretches and exercises to avoid for safety's sake.

Abdominal Strengthening and Endurance

Low back pain and problems usually result from a combination of tight lower back muscles and a lack of abdominal muscle strength. The abdominals work to maintain correct posture and to generate intra-abdominal pressure. This pressure results when the muscle walls around the abdominal cavity are contracted. It helps to support the upper body by taking some of the pressure off the spine. The muscles that need strengthening are the muscles that are diagonally placed around the abdomen. When abdominal exercises are done incorrectly, the hip flexors may be used making the exercise inefficient in strengthening the proper muscles. Abdominal fitness leads to good posture, a must for endurance training and marathoning. This also helps to alleviate low back problems in the rest of your daily activities.

The following series of abdominal conditioning exercises are a fairly standard progression recommended by physical therapists and used by Patti in the exercise classes she teaches.

- **Pelvic Tilts** : For those with little or no abdominal strength. Uses the lower abdominal to tilt pelvis.

Position : Lay on floor with knees bent

Action : Pull lower abdomen in and up making stomach concave. Think of pulling your navel to your backbone. Keep back and buttock muscles relaxed, try to flatten back against the floor. Hold for 5-10 counts.

Progressions : Do 10 tilts per set until you can do 10 sets of ten throughout the day. Tilts can also be done while sitting or while standing against a wall with slightly bent knees.

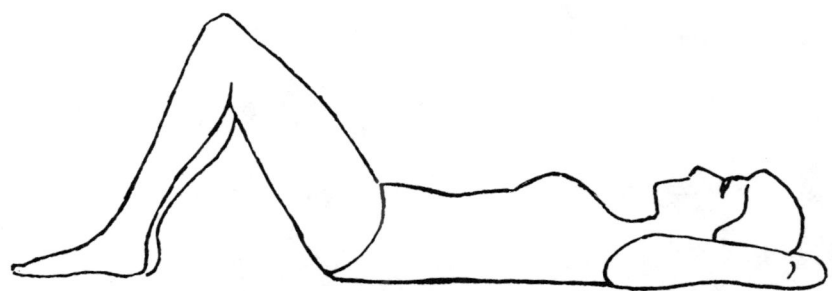

- **Curl Ups**

Position : Lay on the floor with the knees bent.

Action : Do a pelvic tilt. Bring your chin towards your chest and raise your shoulders. Keep stomach concave and curl up one vertebrae at a time.

Progressions : Start with a set of 10. Add 5 repetitions, then 5 more. Add a set of 10, then another. Start with hands as shown in the drawing, hold for five counts. Use arms to come up higher and raise shoulder blades. Hold for 10 counts. Move arm position to change the resistance, cross arms on chest, cross hands behind head, add weight behind head. Add rotation, turn one way, hold 5 counts, turn the other way, hold another 5 counts. Curl up on the diagonal, rotate to the other side, then lower. Do crunches which are curl ups with the feet up on a chair on up against the wall. Final goal is at least 3 sets of 20 with at least one set including rotations.

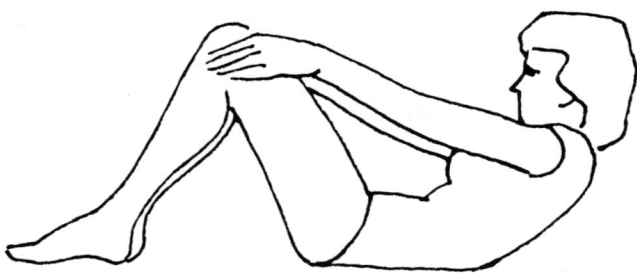

- **Curl Downs**

Position : Sit up with knees bent and slightly more forward than curl ups.

Action : Curl down, bringing tailbone and then lower back in contact with the floor. Keep shoulders rounded forward.

Progressions : Start with sets of 10 as above. Add rotations as shown by rolling over on one hip and raising the opposite shoulder. Work up to 2 sets of 10 one of which includes rotations.

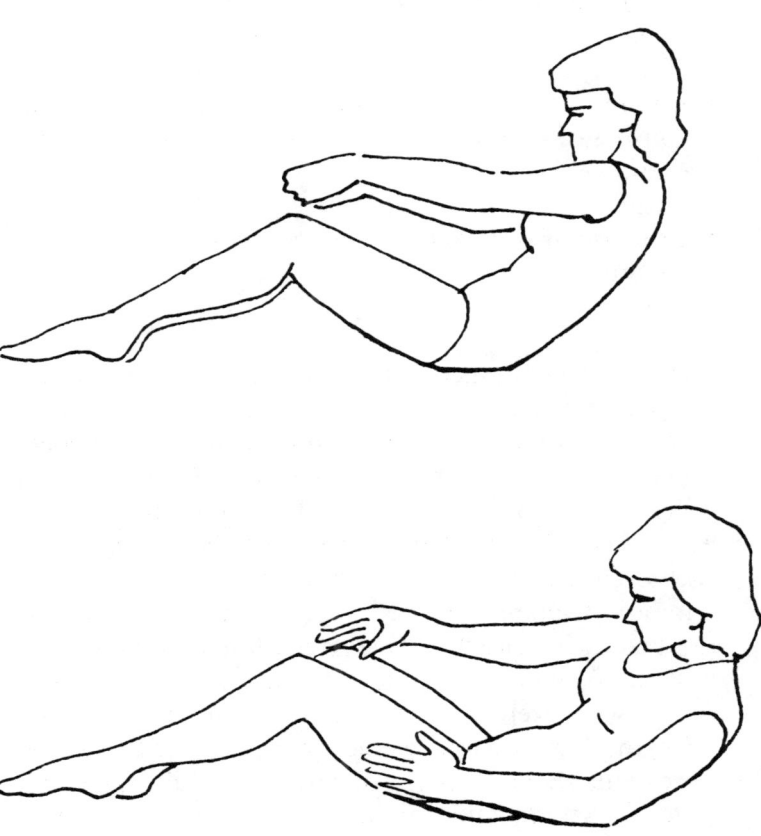

Circuit Weight Training

To understand weight training, you must know some of the basic terminology of exercise and weight training.

- **Weight** : the amount of weight being lifted in the exercise.

- **Repetition (Rep)** : one complete cycle of the exercise. Reps are the number of times the weight is lifted or the number of times the exercise is done.

- **Set** : a group of repetitions, a set consists of a number of repetitions of the exercise or that the weight is lifted.

- **Circuit** : the complete group of exercises. A circuit consists of one set of each of the weight and/or other exercises.

- **Program or workout session** : consists of a number of circuits.

The key to endurance weight training or circuit weight training is performing a number of circuits of many repetitions using low weights. As a contrast a strength program usually consists of 1-3 sets of 8-10 reps of heavy weight for each muscle group. The endurance method has 3-7 circuits of 20-30 reps/set with low weights for each exercise. One study of strength training versus endurance training showed that endurance training resulted in increased muscle strength and endurance as well as maintaining and developing aerobic enzymes in the muscles exercised. The strength training developed strength, but endurance and aerobic muscle enzymes were reduced. The benefits of endurance training include general shaping and toning of the body. Endurance weight training usually does not build big muscle mass. Other benefits are maintenance of body weight and maintenance or reduction of the per cent of body fat. This training can be useful to prevent injury or to rehabilitate after injury. Endurance weight training can be used for cardiovascular training by adding a set of 5 minutes of stationary bicycling or running in place in every circuit. This type of training is often referred to as super circuit training. For runners, this component is usually not necessary.

Weight training can be done with several different kinds of equipment. Free weights such as barbells, dumbbells, ankle and wrist weights or machines such as Universal and Nautilus can be used to great benefit. The program shown here will include instructions for each exercise using inexpensive free weights. A set of dumbbells costs between $10-15 and a set of ankle weights costs about the same. For between $20 and $30, you can have enough equipment at home for a beneficial supplemental training program.

Specific Weight Training

Upper Body Training

During the marathon some of the major fatigue problems occur in the upper body because most runners neglect the training of this area. Arm movement plays an important role in running and follows leg movement. Opposite arms and legs are synchronized in the running stride. The arms absorb reaction from the thrust of the legs. Since action and reaction are interchangeable, arm action may be able to speed up leg action. This action can be useful in running uphill and, more importantly, in maintaining form the last miles of the marathon. When your legs are dragging, you may be able to use your arm movements to lengthen your stride or speed up your leg movement.

Specific exercises will be shown for the following muscles or muscle groups:

- Pectoralis major : pulls the arms forward and across the chest.

- Deltoid : lifts the arms at a right angle to the trunk and assists the arms to move forward and backward.

- Latissimus dorsi : muscle of the upper back which is involved in downward and backward movement of the upper arms.

- Triceps : muscle in the back of the upper arm which extends and straightens the forearms and the elbow joint. Important in the arm swing while running.

- Biceps brachii : muscle in the front of the upper arm which bends the elbow.

- Trapezius : lifts shoulders.

The Exercises

- **Bench Press** : pectorals, deltoids, triceps and Latissimus dorsi.

Lie with back flat, you can bend your knees to keep back flat. Grip dumbbells, barbell or bench press apparatus with overhand grip shoulder width apart. Lift straight up and then lower back to original position. This lift requires a "spotter". A spotter is someone to assist you if you become "out of control" or are in danger of dropping the weight which could land on you in this case.

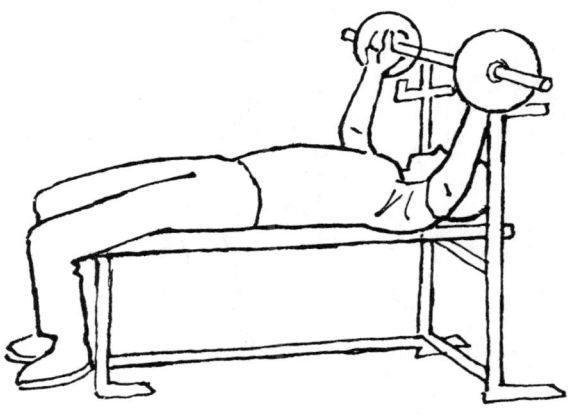

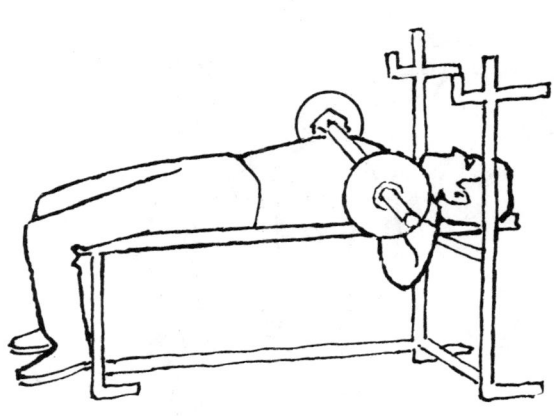

- **Dumbbell Flys** : pectorals, deltoids and Latissimus dorsi.

Lay on back, start with arms extended holding dumbbells up in the air over the face with palms facing. Bring arms down to the sides with wrists cocked and elbows bent 5-10 degrees to relieve stress on the elbow and wrist joints. Return dumbbells to starting position.

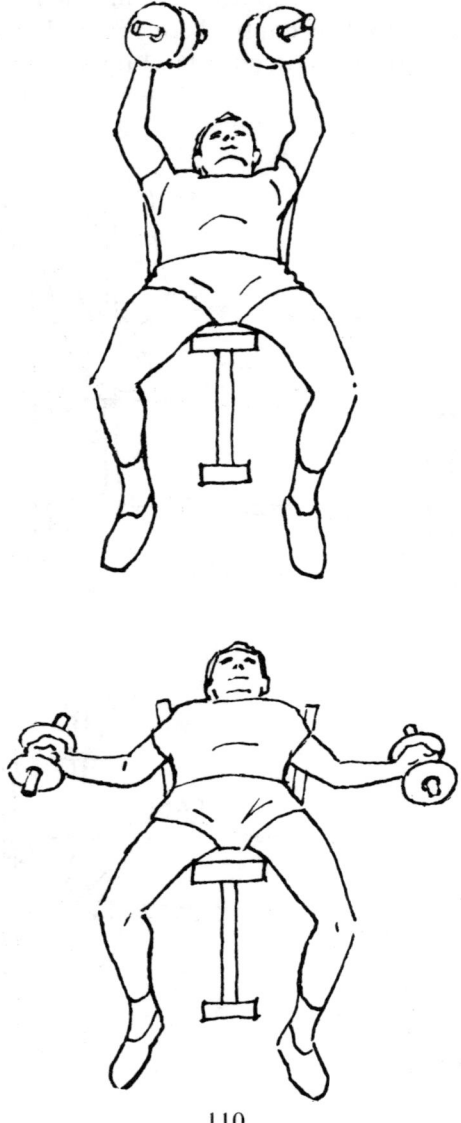

- **Side Lateral Raises** : upper back and rear deltoids.

Stand erect with your feet about shoulder's width apart. Bend slightly forward at the waist. Hold dumbbells in front of groin area with palms toward each other. Keep elbows and wrists slightly bent. Raise dumbbells with palms down straightening the arms, raise to shoulder height. Return to starting position.

- **Bent Lateral Raises** : upper back and rear deltoids.

Stand with knees slightly bent, feet shoulder's width apart. Lean forward, hang arms directly below shoulders with palms facing. Bend arms slightly and raise dumbbells upwards and sideways until level with shoulders. Return to starting position.

- **Triceps Dumbbell Press** : triceps.

Hold dumbbell and arm overhead with wrists locked. The raised arm can be supported with the other hand by holding it at the elbow, armpit or triceps, but does not need to be. Lower the weight behind the head until it touches the shoulder and return to the starting position.

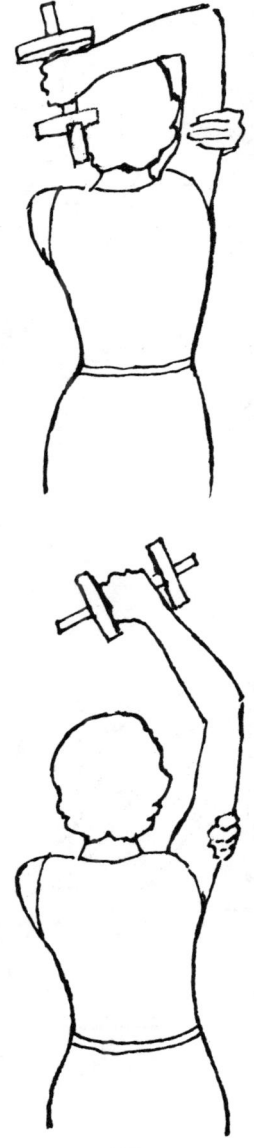

- **Single Arm Dumbbell Rowing** : triceps.

Rest knee on bench. Grasp dumbbell and extend arm downward. Pull up in straight line toward waist. Return to starting position, similar to sawing.

- **Triceps Kickouts**: for triceps.

Take a runner's stance resting one arm on the forward knee. Arm with dumbbell should have elbow bent. Bring elbow up, then extend arm backwards until level with shoulder. Hold for 5 to 10 counts. Return to starting position.

- **Curls** : for biceps.

Grip barbell or dumbbells with an underhanded grip shoulder width apart in either a sitting or standing position. Raise bar or dumbbells to chest and return to starting position. Stand with heels 6 to 8 inches from the wall, bend knees and flatten back against wall to protect the back, do not use back muscles to lift the weight.

Lower Body Training

Exercise will be given for the major groups of muscles in the lower legs. You are already training these muscles, but a little weight training gives even more strength and endurance.

- Quadriceps group : consists of the rectus femoris, vastus intermedius, vastus lateralis and vastus medialis. This group works to extend the knee and flex the hip.

- Hamstrings group : consists of the semimembranosus, semitendinosus and the biceps femoris which work together to flex the leg and rotate the knee.

- Adductor and abductor groups : control inward and outward motion of the leg, rotate the hip and help support the knee. Working on theses muscle will add extra support to the knees, helping to reduce injury.

- **Leg Extensions** : quadriceps group.

These can be done with ankle weights or using a leg extension device on a machine Start in a sitting position, lift the legs onto a horizontal position. Lower only 15 degrees and return to the horizontal. Doing this exercise through the full range of motion is hazardous to the knee. By working only through 15 degrees, the knee is protected from undue stress and the quadriceps are worked. This exercise can also be done by sliding forward on the chair and lifting the straight leg to the horizontal position.

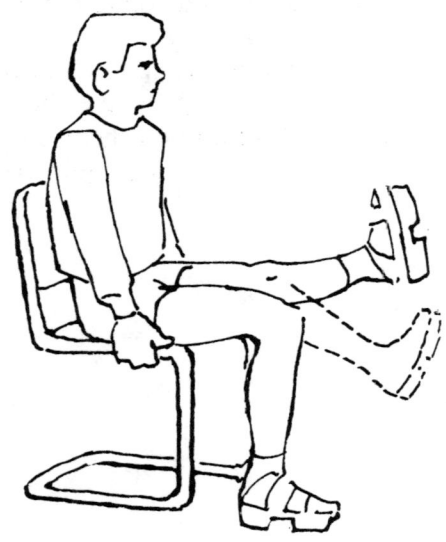

- **Leg Flexions or Curls** : hamstrings group

Lie on bench with knees off the pad. Bring up the legs with the ankle weights, weight shoe or the bar on the machine. Lower to the starting position.

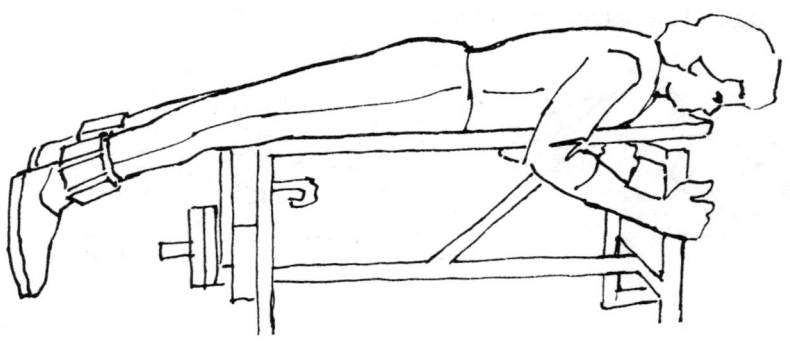

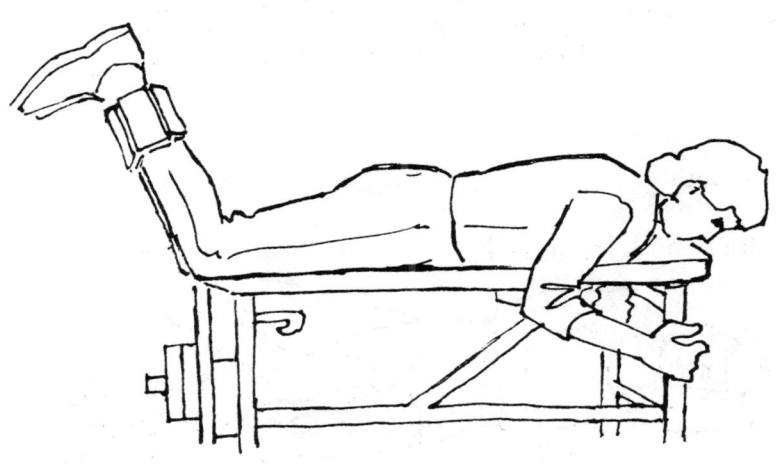

- **Side Leg Raises** : adductors, abductors and secondarily both quads and hamstrings. Excellent for helping knee stability while running.

Lie on the floor on your side with lower arm under your head. Support your weight with your other hand.

- **Bottom Leg**

Bring top leg over and put foot on floor at hip level. Raise lower leg vertically keeping it straight.

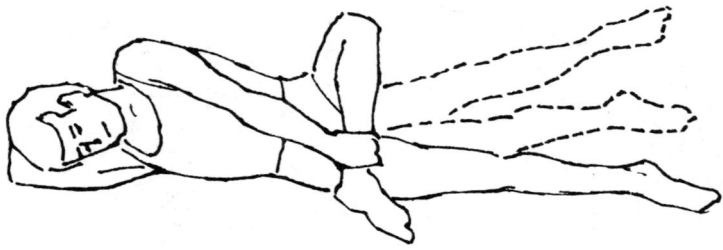

- **Top leg**

Raise leg vertically.

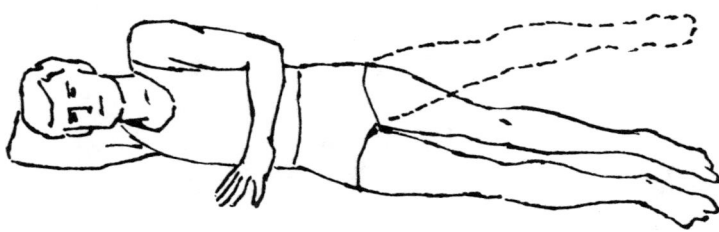

- **Both**

Raise both legs together.

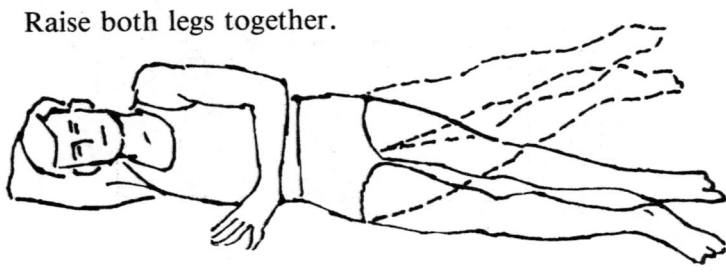

How To Start a Program

1. Pick a set of exercises to compose your circuit. You need not do all of the exercises shown, but choose at least one for each muscle or muscle group. Women should do more than one triceps exercise since they tend to lack upper arm development.

2. Pick the weight you want to lift. Dumbbell progressions for women are 3, 5, 8, to 10 pounds; for men 5, 10, 15, to 20 pounds. Leg progressions are no weight, lift leg alone, 1 ankle weight (Start with 2-2.5 lb, can move to 4-5 lb), 2 ankle weights on same leg.

3. Define the number of repetitions. Increase reps after 3 to 6 sessions. Start with 5 reps to try out the exercise. Do 1 set of 10, add another set of 10. Add 5 reps to each set, add 5 more. Add another set of 20. When you can do at least 3 sets of 20 reps of each exercise in your circuit, then you can add weight. When the weight feels like you can easily lift, you are ready to add either reps or weight. Learn how your body responds to progression. Allow adequate time for compensation by staying 1-2 weeks at each level.

4. Decide on a workout schedule. Weight training works on the same hard/easy principle as running. Hard/easy in weight training is working out one day and then taking the next day off. The best results are obtained by training three days per week, the results are slower with 2 sessions per week. Short term maintenance can be done with 1 workout per week. Each workout should have some warmup and cool down, should include abdominal exercise and should be followed by stretching. Thirty to 40 minutes of weight training per session is adequate.

FOOD AND PERFORMANCE

As you discovered in the physiology section, the source of energy for running is breakdown of the food you eat. Proper intake of food or good nutrition is important for you to gain the benefits of training. A look at general nutrition for the athlete will follow along with some specifics on the relationships of the nutrients to athletic performance.

Human nutrition is thought to require six general classes of nutrients. These are carbohydrates, fats, protein, vitamins, minerals and water. These nutrients are essential for human life and inadequate intake may result in disturbed body metabolism, disease or death. Not all necessary nutrients are contained in any one food and an intake of what is called "a balanced diet", is necessary to achieve adequate nutrition.

Food has three major functions. The first is to provide energy for human metabolism. Carbohydrates and fats are the prime sources of energy. Protein can also provide energy, but that is not its major function. Second, food is used to build and repair body tissues. Protein is the major building material for muscles and other soft tissues while minerals such as calcium and phosphorus are used to build and repair bony tissue. Regulation of body processes is the third use of food. Vitamins, minerals and proteins work together to perform this function. These three functions become increasingly more important to the physically active person. Metabolic activities may increase by tenfold for periods of an hour or longer. Physical performance may be hampered seriously by inadequate nutrition. However, studies on supplemental feeding beyond adequate intake have not revealed an increased capacity for physical performance. The key is to be certain that you are receiving optimal amounts of each specific nutrient recommended by current knowledge of the requirements. Proper nutrition is necessary to optimize energy sources, build and repair tissues, and regulate body processes especially during and following exercise periods.

The four food groups can be a useful guide in taking in the key nutrients. Foods are grouped by similar nutrient values into the Meat Group, the Milk group, the Bread-Cereal Group or the Fruit-Vegetable Group. Eating a wide variety of foods throughout the four food groups helps you to receive an adequate supply of nutrients through a balanced diet. The table below shows the food groups and the recommended minimum servings for adults.

Meat Group	Milk Group	Fruit-Vegetable	Bread-Cereal
2	2	4	4

This approach may have some problems and not be the total solution to a balanced diet. The trend of the American public towards consumption of fats, simple sugars and alcohol led to a Subcommittee of the US Senate to recommend dietary goals for the American public. They are shown on the table below.

	Typical US Diet	**Proposed Diet Goals**
Fat	42%	30%
Saturated	16%	10%
Monounsaturated	13%	10%
Polyunsaturated	13%	10%
Carbohydrate	46%	58%
Simple	24%	10%
Complex	22%	48%
Protein	12%	12%
Cholesterol	500 - 1000 mg	300 mg
Salt	6 - 18 g	3 g

The Human Nutrition Center of the USDA makes the following simple recommendations to help you meet the dietary goals.

- Eat a wide variety of foods from the Basic 4 Food Groups.
- Avoid excessive fat, saturated fat and cholesterol.
- Avoid excessive sodium and salt.
- Avoid excessive amounts of sugar.
- Drink alcohol in moderation.
- Eat foods high in starch and fiber.
- Maintain your ideal body weight.

A good diet is not something you go on, it is simply he way you always eat. The athlete engaged in heavy training should not attempt a weight reduction diet, but may need to change dietary habits to healthy ones. For a more complete treatment at general nutrition, we recommend *Jane Brody's Nutrition Book*. If you are more interested in applications of nutrition to exercise and performance, choose Williams' *Nutrition for Fitness and Sport* or Coleman's *Eating For Endurance*.

Carbohydrates

Carbohydrates (CHO's) are formed when the energy of the sun is harnessed in plants. Simple CHO's are sugars while complex CHO's are many sugars bonded together, known as starches. These are mainly found in plants as is cellulose, a fiber which does not break down in the presence of human digestive enzymes. Cellulose or fiber adds bulk to the diet to prevent constipation and to prevent other problems of the large intestine.

Complex carbohydrates are found mainly in the bread-cereal group and the fruit-vegetable group. Foods such as dry beans, dry peas, milk and ice cream also contain CHO's. Complex rather then simple carbohydrates should be stressed. The US dietary goal is 55-60% for of the total intake be CHO's with simple sugars limited to 15%. The actively training runner may want to have CHO's compose from 55 to 70% of the diet. A study from the E. B. Smith Performance Lab at Texas A&M University showed that of runners who were consuming 25, 50 or 70% carbohydrate diets, only the 70% diet could bring their muscle glycogen back to their pre-exercise level. Other exercise physiologists agree that the high consumption of complex carbohydrates is important for the endurance athlete, but disagree on the exact levels. Coleman in *Eating For Endurance* recommends a 55% level, stating that a higher per cent carbohydrate may influence the body to learn to burn glycogen instead of the desired fat.

Complex CHO's are broken down into simple sugars (glucose and fructose) and absorbed into the blood. Glucose is blood sugar. It may be converted either to liver or muscle glycogen. Liver glycogen can later be converted to blood glucose. The greatest amount of

CHO is stored in the body as muscle glycogen. Excess blood glucose may be stored as fat or may be excreted. It is possible for the body to make blood glucose by liver action from protein and fat, but this metabolism is inefficient and potentially dangerous.

Glucose is the major supplier of energy for the body especially for the brain and muscles. Muscle glycogen in the active muscles is the primary CHO source for energy. As the muscle glycogen is used, blood glucose enters the muscles to maintain muscle glycogen stores and the liver releases some of its glucose to maintain blood sugar levels.

A review of studies on CHO ingestion before and during exercise has led Williams in *Nutrition for Fitness and Sport* to make the following recommendations.

- For individuals on a balanced diet, glucose feedings are unnecessary for continuous exercise bouts lasting 60 to 90 minutes or less. The critical point is to consume adequate amounts of CHO a day or two prior to the event to have adequate storage.

- Ingestion of simple sugar within 1-2 hours before an event may speed up muscle glycogen utilization. This may be a disadvantage for the marathon leading to depletion of muscle glycogen early in the race.

- Glucose feeding may be advisable during events of longer duration at lower speed. The ingested glucose may contribute a significant percentage of CHO energy source helping to spare liver and muscle glycogen supply and prolong the exercise. Marathoners may benefit from glucose feedings and they are most important for ultramarathoners.

The most important concern is always fluid replacement. Too concentrated a solution of glucose may be detrimental because too much sugar in the stomach delays passage of water into the blood stream. Sugar taken shortly before an event may cause overreaction by the pancreas actually leading to a lowering of blood sugar called hypoglycemia. Hypoglycemia can give symptoms of weakness, anxiety and trembling and can contribute to fatigue. Williams offers the following suggestions for glucose solutions taken during exercise.

- If water replacement is the major concern, use only a 1-3% glucose solution.

- If glucose replacement is most important, use a 5-10% solution. Be sure to experiment with the solutions during training before using them in competition. Cola is about a 10% glucose solution and may be diluted according to needs. If the temperature is warm, water replacement is the major concern.

- Homemade solutions can be made using 1 rounded teaspoon of sugar per quart for a 1-2% solution and 3 rounded teaspoons per quart for a 5% solution.

Muscle glycogen stores can be increased by the technique of carbohydrate loading. This is useful for the marathon and requires a switch from a normal balanced diet to one very high in carbohydrate content. Carbohydrate loading is covered under Race Preparation. There you will learn the best method for loading at that time. The training period however is a good time to experiment with your body's response to different carbohydrates eaten in the daily diet and before long runs.

Fats

Fats or lipids is the general term for a number of different compounds found in the body in the form of solid fat or liquid oil. Triglycerides are the primary form in which fats are eaten and stored in the human body. They are composed of fatty acids (FA) attached to a glycerol molecule. The difference between saturated and unsaturated fatty acids concerns the chemical degree of hydrogen saturation of the chemical chain of carbon and hydrogen. Practically speaking, saturated fats are usually solid and are derived from animals, while unsaturated fats are liquid and are derived from vegetables. Fat content in foods can vary from 100% in cooking oils to less than 1% in vegetables. While there is no specific requirement for fat in the diet, there is a need for certain essential FA's that are components of fat. Most are synthesized by the body, but some must be supplied by the diet from polyunsaturated vegetable oils. Sufficient amounts of fat are found in the average diet, in fact, the problem is usually to refrain from ingesting excessive amounts of fat.

Fats are needed to transport certain fat soluble vitamins into the body. Fats are a concentrated energy supply for the body providing 9 calories for every gram making them an easy way to add excess calories to the diet. Fats are used in the diet to make foods taste better by providing flavor, aroma and texture. They satisfy the appetite and delay the return of hunger because they take longer to leave the stomach and be digested. They also dilute the nutrient value of foods by increasing calories without increasing nutrients.

Cholesterol is a fat-like pearly substance called a sterol which is found in animal products. In the human body, cholesterol is manufactured from FA's and the breakdown of CHO and protein. Cholesterol is used in the formation of several hormones and is a component of several tissues. It is vital to human physiology, but since it is manufactured in the body, there is little apparent need to obtain it through food. A relationship has been found between high blood cholesterol levels and coronary heart disease (CHD). The reduction of dietary cholesterol has been advocated by a number of health related organizations for that reason.

Fats are digested mainly in the small intestine recombining into fat droplets in the bloodstream. If you are well fed, the majority of the fat is deposited in the adipose or fat tissue of the body and converted back into triglyceride. The adipose tissue is the body's major energy storage depot and acts as an insulator and shock absorber for various organs. If you are in a fasting state, fat enters the muscle cells where it is either used immediately or stored for future energy use. Your energy balance determines whether fat stores increase or decrease. Excess carbohydrates and proteins are converted by the body to fat and stored in the adipose tissue when food intake is greater than energy output.

The liver regulates the blood lipid level. The lipids in the blood do not circulate as free compounds, but are bound to a protein complex and are known as lipoproteins. These lipoproteins can be grouped into three classes:

- VLDL : very low density lipoproteins - transport triglycerides to the tissues and then become LDL.

- LDL : low density lipoproteins - contain a high proportion of cholesterol and supply this to cells needing it. LDL may be taken up by the cells of the artery walls leading to plaque formation and is implicated in the development of atherosclerosis. "Bad Cholesterol".

- HDL : high density lipoproteins - contain a high proportion of cholesterol, but remove cholesterol from the artery walls and return it to the liver for degradation. HDL associated with lower incidence of coronary heart disease. "Good Cholesterol".

Coronary heart disease is atherosclerosis or plaque formation in the coronary blood vessels which narrows them and reduces blood flow to the heart. A number of risk factors have been found for heart disease. These include improper diet, high serum lipids, high serum cholesterol, physical inactivity, obesity, high blood pressure, smoking, age, heredity, and sex (being male). Dietary modifications have been shown to lower serum cholesterol and triglycerides. These modifications include adjusting caloric intake to maintain ideal body weight, reducing simple sugars and alcohol in the diet and increasing complex CHO's, decreasing dietary cholesterol, and reducing the total amounts of fat in the diet especially animal fats. Diets rich in saturated fat tend to raise serum cholesterol while polyunsaturated fats tend to lower it. Exercise has been shown to increase HDL which may contribute to protection against coronary heart disease. High fat diets have also been implicated in increased risk of breast and colon cancers.

At rest about 60% of the body's energy supply is from fat. Fat is an important source of energy during mild to moderate exercise. The muscles have the oxygen needed to convert energy from the free fatty acids (FFA's) into a form that can be used by the muscles. Fatty acids for energy production can come from the blood stream or from local stores within the muscle. In prolonged mild to moderate exercise, the fat energy stores come mainly from the muscles and from the blood free fatty acids. The adipose tissue keeps supplying FFA's to the bloodstream as it is needed. Fat can supply the majority of energy as long as the exercise remains mild to moderate. As you run faster, the FFA release from adipose tissue slows and the muscle cell begins to rely more and more on CHO as the major energy source. Specific endurance training helps you to become a fat burner at faster paces which helps to spare muscle glycogen.

A physically active person does not need to increase fat intake. Even the leanest runners have adequate fat stores to use as energy and the body can also manufacture fat from carbohydrate and protein. According to the dietary goals, fats should be limited to less than 30% of your diet with saturated fats not more than 10%. Optimally for runners training heavily, fats should comprise less than 20% of the diet to allow consumption of adequate carbohydrates.

Protein

Carbon, hydrogen, oxygen and nitrogen combine to form structures called amino acids. These amino acids are then combined to form the proteins necessary for the structure and functions of the body. The body can form some of the amino acids which are termed nonessential. Those that it cannot are called essential amino acids and must be obtained from the foods in your diet.

The protein found in animal products contains all of the essential amino acids and is called therefore complete protein. These amino acids are also contained in the proper proportions necessary for synthesizing proteins within the body. Protein is found in lesser amounts in plant materials but may be lower in three essential amino acids. Vegetables can be combined to create a complete supply of essential amino acids. Legumes, such as dried beans and peas, provide almost as complete a source of protein as animal foods.

Protein is found in every cell in the body. It has many functions such as the formation of new tissues and the replacement of worn out ones. It also regulates the balance of water, the balance of acids and bases and transports nutrients in and out of cells. Protein forms antibodies, hormones and enzymes. Protein transports nutrients and oxygen in the blood and is essential for blood clotting.

The amount of protein necessary in the diet varies with different life stages with the growth phase requiring the most. The need stabilizes in early adulthood. Throughout the life cycle the protein requirement is based on the weight of the individual. The body needs a new supply of protein every day since excess protein is stored not as amino acids but as fat. Excess intake of protein can lead to increased fat stores and can strain the kidneys in an effort to rid the body of it.

Protein is *not* a major energy source, but excess protein may be converted to carbohydrate or fat. During periods of starvation or semistarvation when adequate amounts of fat and CHO are not available, protein can be utilized for energy. The demand for energy in the body takes precedence over tissue building. The active individual who desires to maintain lean body mass must have adequate fat and CHO calories to spare protein to be used for its more important functions. The dietary goals of 12% allow for adequate protein intake. Many of the common sources of protein are high in fat and calories. Look for animal protein with less fat such as low fat dairy products, poultry and fish, combine small amounts of animal protein with plant sources. Protein insufficiency is one of the major nutritional problems in the world, but the average American consumes about twice as much as is needed per day.

During exercise, protein usually contributes only 1-2% of the energy. Recent research has shown that protein may contribute about 4% of energy demand during prolonged exercise with normal glycogen stores. The percentage may rise to 10% if you are depleted of glycogen, as in the last part of the marathon. CHO loading may have a protein sparing effect for distance runners. The research on whether or not there is destruction of muscular protein during exercise is inconclusive. The amino acid alanine has been found to be released by exercising muscles, but the muscles are also absorbing other amino acids from the blood. Whether there is a net loss of cellular tissue has not been determined. There is little data to support the recommendations of some individuals to increase protein intake during physical training. The overall results show that prolonged low protein intake may have adverse effects on physical performance, but intakes above what is considered normal have not been shown to improve performance.

Vitamins

Vitamins are extremely complex organic compounds found in small amounts in food. They are essential to the optimal functioning of the physiological processes of the human body. Since these processes increase greatly during exercise, an adequate supply of vitamins must be available. Vitamins are essential in human nutrition because of their role in the formation of body enzymes. These enzymes deteriorate over time necessitating a constant fresh supply of vitamins.

Vitamins are not a source of energy and do not have caloric value. They do not contribute to body structure. They are, however, indispensable for regulating body function and for maintenance of optimal health.

Vitamins are divided into 2 classes, fat soluble and water soluble. Fat soluble vitamins include Vitamins A, D, E and K. Some essential water soluble vitamins are Vitamins B1, B2, Niacin, B6, Pantothenic Acid, Folacin, B12, Biotin, Choline, Inositol, and C. Fat soluble vitamins are stored in the body to a greater degree than water soluble vitamins. Most vitamins must be obtained from food, a few are formed within the body.

The only difference between natural and synthetic vitamins is the way they are made. Usually it is better to get vitamins from food because they are in combination with minerals and other nutrients needed by the body. Synthetic vitamins may be indicated when deficiencies are noted. Most nutritionists feel that there is no evidence that the average American on a balanced diet suffers from vitamin deficiency. Little evidence exists to support the use of vitamin supplements by well nourished athletes or other highly active persons. However, Charles A. Garfield based on his research at the Performance Sciences Institute indicates that vitamin and mineral supplements can be important in the nutrition of competitors. He concludes that athletes can benefit from

2 multivitamin tablets with minerals per day. He also suggest extra amounts of Vitamin C (2,000-5,000 mg) and B Complex are advisable during strenuous training periods. His study of marathoners given the above vitamin supplements showed a drop in resting heart rates of 9 beats per minute while no significant changes were shown in a control group. Runners taking the supplements experienced 35% fewer injuries and 81% fewer infections than the control group. If you feel that you are not receiving a balanced diet for any reason, reasonable doses of vitamin supplements will not be harmful. However, excess quantities or megadoses can have undesirable side effects and are dangerous. A registered dietitian can answer more detailed questions regarding vitamin intake.

Minerals

A mineral is a solid inorganic element found in nature. Twenty five of the elements are essential in humans and have a wide variety of functions. Some are used as building blocks for body tissues while others are important components of enzymes and hormones. Others regulate the physiologic processes of the body. The six major minerals are calcium, phosphorus, sodium, potassium, chloride and magnesium. The relationship of some of these major minerals to running will be discussed.

Inadequate intake of calcium by adults can result in a loss of bone density and in muscle cramps. Many experts believe that an adequate intake of calcium is between 1000 and 1500 milligrams per day. Good sources of dietary calcium are low fat dairy products, dried beans and many vegetables, especially green leafy ones. Calcium needs Vitamin D to be absorbed which should pose no problems to those who run outdoors most days.

Iron is important for the transport of oxygen. Iron deficiency is sometimes found in women of child bearing age, vegetarians and endurance athletes who ingest little animal-based protein. Better iron absorption from the dietary sources of meat, poultry and fish is obtained when these are combined with Vitamin C rich fruit or vegetables.

Sodium and chloride combine to form common table salt. Excess salt consumption has been linked to hypertension. The average American consumes about 2-4 teaspoons of salt per day. The suggested daily allotment, far in excess of actual need, is set at between 1-2 teaspoons per day. Enough sodium is naturally present in foods to meet the daily requirements of everyone with the possible exception of those who exercise strenuously in hot weather. If you are running in the heat, you should not restrict your salt intake unless advised to do so by your physician. If you lose over three quarts of sweat, (6 pounds of body weight), you should add 1/3 to 1 teaspoon of salt to the diet for every quart of sweat lost (2 pounds weight). Salt tablets are not recommended because they provide too concentrated a salt form which can impair athletic performance by drawing water out of the functioning muscle cells.

Water

Water, the most important nutrient, is a compound composed of 2 parts hydrogen and one part oxygen. Water provides no food energy or calories, but is needed by every cell to carry out essential functions.

About two thirds of the body weight is water with the majority being within the cells. Water is the main transport mechanism within the body for carrying oxygen, nutrients and hormones to the cells and removing waste products. The waste products are eliminated from the body through the water in sweat, urine and feces. Water also regulates osmotic pressure controlling the proper electrolyte balance and acid/base balance. Water lubricates and cushions. It acts as the body's main cooling system.

The requirement for water depends on the weight and age of the individual, but the average adult needs about

2 quarts of water a day to maintain water balance within the body. The balance is maintained when intake of water matches output of body fluids. The main output for water is urine, however, some is lost in the feces and some through exhaled air. Insensible perspiration, which cannot be seen, is a significant source of body water loss. Sweat losses increase greatly with exercise or hot environmental conditions.

The major source of water is fluid intake. Solid foods also contribute through their water content and through metabolism of these foods for energy. Fat, CHO and protein produce water known as metabolic water when broken down for energy.

Normal levels of body water are maintained through kidney function. Loss of body water results in conservation by the kidneys while increased consumption leads to the kidneys ridding the body of excess water. Your body usually lets you know when you need water by thirst. In normal conditions, thirst is usually a good guide to body water needs and is effective in restoring body water to normal. Thirst is not a good indicator of body needs during exercise and especially when exercising in hot weather.

ERGOGENIC AIDS

Athletes are often searching for ways to gain a competitive "edge". Substances that are used to increase physical work capacity, or in this case, improve performance are termed ergogenic aids.

Water and Other Fluids

Taking fluid aid during the marathon is a valuable help to good performance. The most important need during the marathon is for water replacement. Water must be replaced as it is used during the run. Water replenishment is especially important when running in the heat. (See Food and Performance) Practice drinking during your training runs so that you are accustomed to running with liquid in your stomach and so that you can learn how to get it in. While running the marathon, begin taking water at the first aid station. Drink at least one cup, preferably 2. If it is hot, pour another one over your head and shoulders. If you cannot drink while running, slow down and walk while you drink. The few seconds lost while drinking will easily be made up by feeling good throughout the race because you are well hydrated. Drink 1-2 cups at every aid station. Do not use thirst as a regulator of intake as the feeling of thirst does not keep up with the exercising body's need for water replacement. Water taken in after about the 22 mile point will probably not be used. However, the short rest and the psychological boost of a drink at that point may be important.

Other types of drinks containing glucose and electrolytes are discussed in Running in Temperature Extremes. Generally, it is not necessary to replace electrolytes during the event, but they should be replaced afterwards. Glucose ingestion has been shown to be useful in events of over 1-1/2 to 2 hours such as the marathon. During the race, you usually have a choice of water and a glucose electrolyte solution.

If you plan to drink the offered solution, purchase the same brand before the race and use it during your training runs. Never drink an unknown or untried solution during the race. Always take water with the solution that is offered because the body's greatest need is for water and the solution offered may be improperly mixed for optimal absorption. Too much sugar slows down the absorption of water from the stomach and too high concentration of electrolytes may cause intestinal cramps. If you have problems drinking on the run or if the temperature is warmer than normal, you may benefit from hyperhydration. Drink a pint (2 cups) or more of water 15-30 minutes before the run. Practice this on training runs as well. Keep in mind that the water combined with pre-race nervousness may force you to stay close to the restrooms.

Carbohydrate loading is an ergogenic aid for events longer than 2 hours such as the marathon. A suggested method of loading in conjunction with tapering is discussed in the Race Preparation Section.

Steroids and Amphetamines

The American College of Sports Medicine has issued a position statement on anabolic and androgenic steroids after a careful analysis of the available literature. The College states that these steroids in approved therapeutic doses do not bring any significant improvements in strength, aerobic endurance, lean body mass or body weight. There is no evidence that large doses either aid or hinder performance. The drugs have many dangerous side effects making them *unsafe* to use.

Amphetamines or "pep pills" are also not indicated for usage in athletics. These pills are often taken by athletes to be "up" or psychologically ready. This is usually unnecessary and may have dangerous effects such as drug dependency and side effects such as headache, dizziness and masking the body's perception of pain, fatigue and heat stress which can actually hinder performance.

Caffeine

Although caffeine has no food value, it may be the only stimulant of value in endurance running. It acts as a central nervous system, heart rate and force stimulant, a smooth muscle relaxant, a stimulant for the release of adrenalin and will increase the amount of fatty acids in the blood. It may also increase the secretion of stomach acids and can act as a diuretic. Some recent research has shown that caffeine may be beneficial to performance in events lasting longer than 2 hours, such as the marathon. The caffeine elevates the free fatty acids in the blood and increases their utilization by the muscle for energy during the run. This action decreases the amount of muscle glycogen used, sparing muscle glycogen so that it can used better throughout the entire run. This benefit may only occur in certain individuals and caffeine drinks should be tried on training runs to discover your personal reaction. Certain individuals have strong adverse reactions to caffeine and should not use it.

Alcohol

Alcohol does not seem to provide useful energy during exercise and may adversely effect physiologic processes important to energy metabolism during exercise. As a depressant, it may adversely effect perceptual-motor activities. The results of one or two drinks probably do not have any serious negative effects on performance, but recent studies have shown that during long distance running, alcohol may block the formation of glucose by the liver and decrease the release of glucose from the stomach. These actions may result in a decrease in blood glucose during the latter stages of the marathon. The most detrimental action is the disturbance of water balance in the muscle cells which could lead to a disturbance of cell enzyme activity with resultant increased fatigue. Light to moderate social drinking the evening prior to the event, but not on the same day, has not been shown to adversely effect physical performance. Overindulgence the night before may have the adverse effects listed above during the race if the alcohol has not been cleared from the system. Save the drinking of alcoholic beverages until after the race as your reward for a race well run.

Aspirin

Aspirin may or may not be an ergogenic aid. Neither aspirin nor any other drug should be taken to mask specific pain before beginning a race. If something hurts enough to require aspirin, you should consider not running, waiting for the next marathon and sparing your body pain and injury. The anti-inflammatory effect of aspirin to reduce swelling can be helpful over the long term. Too much aspirin can block you from receiving the messages that your body needs to stop, can lead to problems with heat adaptation, can lead to ringing in the ears and stomach discomfort. One to two aspirins an hour before the race can give you anti-inflammatory effects during the race. Never take aspirin before or during the race if you've never done it in training. The combined effects of aspirin and caffeine on an empty stomach can be devastating by causing pain and nausea.

Blood Doping

Blood cell re-infusion or "doping" has been in the news after several Olympics. A controversy from the 1984 Olympics was the use of this technique by the American bicycling team.

The procedure consists of withdrawing a pint of an individual's blood 6-8 weeks before the event. That blood is stored and reinfused into the individual 1-2 days before the event. In the interim, the individual has restored normal red blood cell level. The added blood cells and volume are theorized to contribute to a larger maximal heart output and increase the oxygen carrying capacity of the blood. It is actually possible that doping may have opposite effects. The increase in the red blood cells could make the blood thicker and therefore, harder to pump through the body. Studies have not shown any real evidence that the procedure works. The major problem with this technique deals with its ethical considerations and the health problems that could result if the individual is infused with blood from an unknown donor. We mention it here namely for your understanding of the process, but strongly discourage anyone from attempting it. You will increase your performance to a greater degree through intelligent training than you can through any techniques such as blood doping.

RUNNING IN TEMPERATURE EXTREMES

Performance may be influenced tremendously by temperature. As air temperature rises, the combination of environmental heat and increased body heat from exercise may result in bad effects ranging from decreased performance to death. Extreme cold, while usually not life threatening, can cause excessive body heat loss making good performance difficult.

The human body is able to maintain a fairly constant temperature under varying environmental conditions. To do this, it must be able to gain or lose heat. The core temperature is regulated to remain relatively constant, but the temperature of the shell, the skin and the tissues directly beneath it, varies directly with environmental conditions. The hypothalamus in the brain controls the body temperature and calls into play either heat loss or heat production mechanisms. Regulation comes in response to changes in the skin or blood temperature.

Normal metabolism in the body produces heat. Increased heat production can come from higher metabolic rates, disease, shivering or exercise. During exercise, the increased metabolic rate and energy production both generate heat. Most of the heat gain is due to the lack of efficiency of the body. It converts only 20-25% of energy produced into work; the rest is dissipated as heat.

Heat loss is governed by the following physical means.

- **Conduction** : transfer of heat from the body by direct physical contact.

- **Convection** : transfer of heat by movement of air or water over the body.

- **Radiation** : radiation of heat from the body into space.

- **Evaporation** : loss of heat by the body when converting sweat to vapor.

In a cold or cool environment, conduction and convection, along with some evaporation of sweat, can maintain the heat balance. As the temperature rises, evaporation of sweat becomes the main way of controlling the rise in core temperature. Evaporation can keep the body's exercising temperature in the normal range of 102-105 F under normal environmental circumstances.

Four environmental factors can interact to change the effectiveness of evaporation mechanism. They are air temperature, relative humidity, air movement, and radiation. Caution should be advised when the temperature is above 80 F or when the relative humidity exceeds 50-60%. A small breeze will help keep the body temperature near normal by helping to evaporate sweat. Radiant heat absorbed from the sun by the body will add to the heat load.

Heat Illnesses

Running unwisely under environmental heat stress may lead to a variety of heat illnesses which can be life threatening. These illnesses are caused by three factors: increased core temperature, loss of body fluids, and loss of electrolytes. While running in the heat, monitor your condition for signs of weakness, dizziness, nausea, disorientation, cessation of sweating and piloerection, the standing up of body hairs. If these signs occur, stop running and start the appropriate treatment. They could be symptoms of any of the major heat illnesses described below.

- **Heat Cramps** : Salts can be lost in the sweat while running in the heat. If they are not replenished properly, muscle pain and cramps can occur. The body temperature does not become elevated. Prevention can come from heat acclimatization, ingestion of large amounts of water and by increasing the daily salt intake several days before the heat stress. Treatment is rest in a cool environment and replacement of lost salts.

- **Heat Exhaustion** : Poor circulatory response to heat and reduction of blood volume due to increased sweating can lead to symptoms of general weakness, dizziness and nausea. The skin is usually cool and pale, but the person is probably still sweating. Body temperature is not elevated to dangerous levels (under 106F). Exercise must be stopped. Treat by rest in a cool environment, ingestion of cool liquids and cooling the body externally with water or ice.

- **Heat Stroke** : When the body's temperature regulating system fails, excessively high body temperature and heat stroke can result. This is a serious condition which, if untreated, may well lead to death. It requires *immediate* medical attention. The symptoms are dry, warm and red skin, a reduction or loss of sweat and a body core temperature over 106F. Treatment is to immediately stop exercise, seek medical attention and start cooling the body with ice packs and cold water. The person may or may not be conscious. Cool liquids may be consumed if the person is conscious.

There are ways to reduce hazards when running in the heat and/or humidity, most are common sense:

- Check the conditions before exercising and adjust your plan if needed. Slow the pace or decrease the duration of activity if training when hot or humid. If racing when hot and humid, realize that performance will less than expected. If the event is not a key one, relax and save the bigger effort for a cooler day.

- Run in the early morning or late evening to avoid the heat of the day. In many climates, late afternoon is the hottest time of the day and running then should be avoided.

- Find a shady road or trail to run on.

- Dress accordingly, wear as few clothes as you decently can. Try loose fitting white shorts and a white mesh top to reflect the heat and to permit evaporation. Protect your head from intense sun with a lightweight hat that can breathe. The back of the neck can be protected by the hat or a cotton kerchief. Ice can be wrapped in the kerchief and carried under the hat.

- Drink fluids while running. Carry a water bottle or pick a route with water fountains. Drink 6-8 oz. of water for every 15-20 minutes of running. Also pour water over your head and chest.

- Weigh yourself daily and replenish lost water. Body weight should be back to normal before the next workout.

- Try hyperhydration by drinking 2-4 cups of water 30 minutes before running.

- Be aware of lost electrolytes if you've sweated excessively. Put an appropriate amount salt on foods and eat bananas and citrus fruit.

- Avoid excess protein intake. Protein metabolism produces extra heat.

- Know the signs and symptoms of heat illness and their treatments. If you have any of the symptoms, stop running, get to a cool place and consume cold fluids.

- If you are going to compete in an event in hot conditions, acclimatize first.

Heat Acclimatization

Acclimatization is the process of adapting your body to be able to run more efficiently under hot environmental conditions. When it is hot the blood goes to the skin for cooling the body as well as to the working muscles. This increases the workload of the heart and the exercising heart rate. Intensity of exercise will need to be reduced when running in the heat and when acclimatizing for proper adaptation.

The body makes several adjustments during the heat acclimatization process. The circulatory adaptations to acclimatization provide better transport of heat from the core to the skin. There is better distribution of the blood to regulate temperature. This frees a greater portion of the heart output for the working muscles. Sweating mechanisms undergo complementary changes. Sweating starts at a lower body temperature and the capacity for sweating nearly doubles. The sweat becomes more dilute, contains less salt, and is more evenly distributed over the skin. Major changes occur during the first week of heat exposure and are mostly complete after 10 days.

The ways to acclimatize are:

- Begin early in the season when the temperature is moderate and wear one more layer of clothing than usual on 3 runs per week. If you would normally wear a T-shirt wear a long sleeved one or a jacket. This technique provides a hot, humid microatmosphere and prevents evaporation. This early constant acclimatization works well in climates such as in Oregon where the weather is often unpredictable and occasional hot days are experienced relatively early in the year.

- If the weather suddenly turns hot, reduce the training load; run slower and less distance. Slowly build back up to usual mileage and intensity. Work on heat acclimatization every other day and make certain to replace lost fluids. Run in the cooler part of the day on the nonacclimatization days. Do not overdo and get heat symptoms.

- If you plan to race under hot conditions, remember that acclimatization takes about 10 days. Plan to be acclimatized a week in advance. During the week before the event, avoid extra heat stress which may dehydrate and fatigue you for the race.

Fluid and Electrolyte Replacement

Optimal performance depends on proper hydration. Dehydration or excessive loss of body water reduces the amount of time you can exercise as well as necessitating slowing down. Changes that take place at the cellular level adversely effect muscle contraction. Water losses of 2% or more of body weight impair circulatory function and create heat imbalance.

Sweat is comprised mainly of water and sodium and chloride ions. These ions are known as electrolytes. Other electrolytes are also present in small amounts. Studies of electrolyte balance during and after exercise have shown increases in the electrolytes in the blood, but these changes are probably due to water loss and muscle use.

Electrolyte deficiency probably does not occur during marathon running. It is during the recovery period after prolonged sweating when the content of electrolytes in the blood has been shown to be lower. Electrolytes should be replaced following the run. Studies of marathon running have shown that the most important factor is to replace body water lost during the run. Small amounts of glucose taken throughout the run may be helpful as well.

If running in the heat for several consecutive days, try to replace fluids and eat a balanced diet. Add salt to foods and select foods high in potassium such as bananas and citrus fruits. Salt tablets are unnecessary and may be harmful when not taken with adequate water.

Replacement Drinks

There has been no evidence to show that glucose-electrolyte solutions help replenish body water better than plain water. Electrolytes do not need replacing during exercise. After exercise, replenish as noted above. Glucose might be useful during exercise, but the concentration of the solution is very important and differs depending on the temperature. Too high a sugar concentration will retard absorption of water and too high electrolyte concentration tends to lead to intestinal cramps. If you plan to take any of these substances during a race, experiment during training before doing so. During high intensity prolonged exercise in the heat fluid replacement drinks:

- Should contain less than 1.5 rounded teaspoons of sugar per quart.

- Should contain little, if any, electrolytes.

- Should be cold (40-50 F).

You should drink 6-8 ounces of fluid every 15-20 minutes during exercise. You can also hyperhydrate by drinking 2-4 cups of cold fluid 15-30 minutes before exercise.

Running in the Cold

Cold is usually not as hazardous for the runner as is heat. With exercise metabolism, the body is able to maintain a constant core temperature in air temperatures as low as -22F. This is regulated by internal mechanisms and not necessarily by the heat produced from exercise. Shivering can be seen during exercise when the core temperature is low. Under this stress, oxygen consumption is higher than when doing the same amount of exercise in warm weather.

Common sense tells you to be comfortable while running; this is also true in cold weather. Both body fat and clothing act as heat conserving mechanisms. High body fat is not conducive to good performance and is not common in runners, so most must learn to dress warmly. Layers of clothing trap and warm air between them to act as insulation. If clothing becomes wet either through sweating or external sources (rain, snow), it can conduct heat away from the body. Fabrics that are waterproof, but can still breathe are best for external layers. Polypropylene is excellent next to the skin as it wicks away the water and allows a warm air layer to remain. A major part of heat loss is through the head, so wear a hat or ski headband to help keep warm. Gloves are nice as well. You can remove gloves, hat or layers of clothing as you become warmer. Running with bare legs in cold weather is not advised. The red color of the skin shows that a great deal of the blood is detoured to the skin trying to keep the body warm and is not going to the exercising muscles where it is needed most. Cold muscles feel tight and are more susceptible to injury, especially pulls and strains.

APPENDICES

EXAMPLE TRAINING LOG

A simple training log is useful for laying out your program and monitoring your progress. The one given below is used in the Portland Marathon Clinic. You can devise a similar form of your own. If you lay out one on a single sheet of paper you can copy it and use a loose leaf notebook to store enough weeks for your entire training plan. Fill out your workout schedules several weeks into the future, planning around things such as races, appointments etc..

Each day log your resting pulse (HR), your weight, general health (1-5 scale), and when you went to bed. After your workout log your recovery pulse (HR), time and any other comments. You can refer to your log to monitor your progress, to determine where things went right or wrong or to look for signs of overtraining.

Workout Schedule for:	**Week of:**
SUN Pulse: Weight: Health: Bed Hr:	Comments:
MON Pulse: Weight: Health: Bed Hr:	Comments:
TUE Pulse: Weight: Health: Bed Hr:	Comments:
WED Pulse: Weight: Health: Bed Hr:	Comments:
THU Pulse: Weight: Health: Bed Hr:	Comments:
FRI Pulse: Weight: Health: Bed Hr:	Comments:
SAT Pulse: Weight: Health: Bed Hr:	Comments:

TRAINING PACE TABLES

The following tables are provided for determining appropriate training paces for runners of various abilities. Each table contains:

- A realistic marathon goal and pace

- An estimated maximum aerobic pace

- "Easy" training speeds from 2-25 miles

The easy training paces can be used as a guide during the base building phases of training and for rest and recovery runs. These paces represent the 75-80% effort range.

Marathon goal pace is not only useful for planning splits, but can be used for pace training speeds (i.e. *tempo runs*).

The maximum aerobic pace is given for use by advanced runners in developing interval workouts.

Training Paces for 28 Minute 10K Runner

(2:10 Marathon Goal)

Marathon Goal Pace: 4:59 per mile

Max Aerobic Pace: 1:01 per 440 yds

Miles	Time	Easy Run Paces: (min)	Pace(min/mi)	
2	10:24	11:05	5:12	5:32
3	16:03	17:07	5:21	5:42
4	21:50	23:18	5:27	5:49
5	27:44	29:35	5:32	5:55
6	33:42	35:57	5:37	5:59
7	39:45	42:24	5:40	6:03
8	45:51	48:55	5:43	6:06
9	52:01	55:29	5:46	6:09
10	58:13	1:02:06	5:49	6:12
11	1:04:29	1:08:46	5:51	6:15
12	1:10:46	1:15:29	5:53	6:17
13	1:17:06	1:22:14	5:55	6:19
14	1:23:28	1:29:01	5:57	6:21
15	1:29:51	1:35:51	5:59	6:23
16	1:36:17	1:42:42	6:01	6:25
17	1:42:44	1:49:35	6:02	6:26
18	1:49:13	1:56:30	6:04	6:28
19	1:55:43	2:03:26	6:05	6:29
20	2:02:15	2:10:24	6:06	6:31
21	2:08:48	2:17:23	6:08	6:32
22	2:15:22	2:24:24	6:09	6:33
23	2:21:58	2:31:26	6:10	6:35
24	2:28:35	2:38:29	6:11	6:36
25	2:35:13	2:45:34	6:12	6:37

Training Paces for 30 Minute 10K Runner

(2:20 Marathon Goal)

Marathon Goal Pace: 5:20 per mile

Max Aerobic Pace: 1:05 per 440 yds

Miles	Easy Run Paces: Time (min)		Pace (min/mi)	
2	11:08	11:53	5:34	5:56
3	17:12	18:21	5:44	6:07
4	23:24	24:57	5:51	6:14
5	29:43	31:41	5:56	6:20
6	36:07	38:31	6:01	6:25
7	42:35	45:26	6:05	6:29
8	49:08	52:24	6:08	6:33
9	55:44	59:27	6:11	6:36
10	1:02:23	1:06:33	6:14	6:39
11	1:09:05	1:13:41	6:16	6:41
12	1:15:49	1:20:53	6:19	6:44
13	1:22:36	1:28:07	6:21	6:46
14	1:29:25	1:35:23	6:23	6:48
15	1:36:16	1:42:41	6:25	6:50
16	1:43:09	1:50:02	6:26	6:52
17	1:50:04	1:57:25	6:28	6:54
18	1:57:01	2:04:49	6:30	6:56
19	2:03:59	2:12:15	6:31	6:57
20	2:10:59	2:19:43	6:32	6:59
21	2:18:00	2:27:12	6:34	7:00
22	2:25:02	2:34:43	6:35	7:01
23	2:32:06	2:42:15	6:36	7:03
24	2:39:12	2:49:48	6:38	7:04
25	2:46:18	2:57:23	6:39	7:05

Training Paces for 32 Minute 10K Runner

(2:29 Marathon Goal)

Marathon Goal Pace: 5:41 per mile

Max Aerobic Pace: 1:10 per 440 yds

Miles	Time	Easy Run Paces: (min)	Pace (min/mi)	
2	11:53	12:41	5:56	6:20
3	18:21	19:34	6:07	6:31
4	24:57	26:37	6:14	6:39
5	31:41	33:48	6:20	6:45
6	38:31	41:05	6:25	6:50
7	45:26	48:27	6:29	6:55
8	52:24	55:54	6:33	6:59
9	59:27	1:03:25	6:36	7:02
10	1:06:33	1:10:59	6:39	7:05
11	1:13:41	1:18:36	6:41	7:08
12	1:20:53	1:26:16	6:44	7:11
13	1:28:07	1:33:59	6:46	7:13
14	1:35:23	1:41:45	6:48	7:16
15	1:42:41	1:49:32	6:50	7:18
16	1:50:02	1:57:22	6:52	7:20
17	1:57:25	2:05:14	6:54	7:22
18	2:04:49	2:13:08	6:56	7:23
19	2:12:15	2:21:04	6:57	7:25
20	2:19:43	2:29:02	6:59	7:27
21	2:27:12	2:37:01	7:00	7:28
22	2:34:43	2:45:02	7:01	7:30
23	2:42:15	2:53:04	7:03	7:31
24	2:49:48	3:01:08	7:04	7:32
25	2:57:23	3:09:13	7:05	7:34

Training Paces for 34 Minute 10K Runner

(2:38 Marathon Goal)

Marathon Goal Pace: 6:03 per mile

Max Aerobic Pace: 1:14 per 440 yds

Miles	Time	Easy Run Paces: (min)	Pace	(min/mi)
2	12:38	13:28	6:19	6:44
3	19:29	20:47	6:29	6:55
4	26:31	28:17	6:37	7:04
5	33:40	35:55	6:44	7:11
6	40:56	43:39	6:49	7:16
7	48:16	51:29	6:53	7:21
8	55:41	59:24	6:57	7:25
9	1:03:10	1:07:22	7:01	7:29
10	1:10:42	1:15:25	7:04	7:32
11	1:18:18	1:23:31	7:07	7:35
12	1:25:56	1:31:40	7:09	7:38
13	1:33:37	1:39:52	7:12	7:40
14	1:41:21	1:48:06	7:14	7:43
15	1:49:07	1:56:23	7:16	7:45
16	1:56:55	2:04:42	7:18	7:47
17	2:04:45	2:13:04	7:20	7:49
18	2:12:37	2:21:27	7:22	7:51
19	2:20:31	2:29:53	7:23	7:53
20	2:28:27	2:38:20	7:25	7:55
21	2:36:24	2:46:50	7:26	7:56
22	2:44:23	2:55:20	7:28	7:58
23	2:52:23	3:03:53	7:29	7:59
24	3:00:25	3:12:27	7:31	8:01
25	3:08:29	3:21:03	7:32	8:02

Training Paces for 36 Minute 10K Runner

(2:48 Marathon Goal)

Marathon Goal Pace: 6:24 per mile

Max Aerobic Pace: 1:19 per 440 yds

Miles	Time	Easy Run Paces: (min)	Pace(min/mi)	
2	13:22	14:16	6:41	7:08
3	20:38	22:01	6:52	7:20
4	28:05	29:57	7:01	7:29
5	35:39	38:02	7:07	7:36
6	43:20	46:14	7:13	7:42
7	51:06	54:31	7:18	7:47
8	58:58	1:02:53	7:22	7:51
9	1:06:53	1:11:20	7:25	7:55
10	1:14:52	1:19:51	7:29	7:59
11	1:22:54	1:28:26	7:32	8:02
12	1:30:59	1:37:03	7:34	8:05
13	1:39:08	1:45:44	7:37	8:08
14	1:47:18	1:54:28	7:39	8:10
15	1:55:32	2:03:14	7:42	8:12
16	2:03:47	2:12:03	7:44	8:15
17	2:12:05	2:20:54	7:46	8:17
18	2:20:25	2:29:47	7:48	8:19
19	2:28:47	2:38:42	7:49	8:21
20	2:37:11	2:47:39	7:51	8:22
21	2:45:36	2:56:38	7:53	8:24
22	2:54:03	3:05:39	7:54	8:26
23	3:02:32	3:14:42	7:56	8:27
24	3:11:02	3:23:46	7:57	8:29
25	3:19:34	3:32:52	7:58	8:30

Training Paces for 38 Minute 10K Runner

(2:57 Marathon Goal)

Marathon Goal Pace: 6:45 per mile

Max Aerobic Pace: 1:23 per 440 yds

Miles	Time	Easy Run Paces: (min)	Pace(min/mi)	
2	14:07	15:03	7:03	7:31
3	21:47	23:14	7:15	7:44
4	29:38	31:37	7:24	7:54
5	37:38	40:09	7:31	8:01
6	45:45	48:48	7:37	8:08
7	53:57	57:33	7:42	8:13
8	1:02:14	1:06:23	7:46	8:17
9	1:10:36	1:15:18	7:50	8:22
10	1:19:01	1:24:17	7:54	8:25
11	1:27:30	1:33:20	7:57	8:29
12	1:36:03	1:42:27	8:00	8:32
13	1:44:38	1:51:37	8:02	8:35
14	1:53:16	2:00:49	8:05	8:37
15	2:01:57	2:10:05	8:07	8:40
16	2:10:40	2:19:23	8:10	8:42
17	2:19:26	2:28:43	8:12	8:44
18	2:28:13	2:38:06	8:14	8:47
19	2:37:03	2:47:31	8:15	8:49
20	2:45:54	2:56:58	8:17	8:50
21	2:54:48	3:06:27	8:19	8:52
22	3:03:43	3:15:58	8:21	8:54
23	3:12:40	3:25:31	8:22	8:56
24	3:21:39	3:35:06	8:24	8:57
25	3:30:39	3:44:42	8:25	8:59

Training Paces for 40 Minute 10K Runner

(3:06 Marathon Goal)

Marathon Goal Pace: 7:07 per mile

Max Aerobic Pace: 1:27 per 440 yds

Miles	Easy Run Paces: Time (min)		Pace (min/mi)	
2	14:51	15:51	7:25	7:55
3	22:56	24:28	7:38	8:09
4	31:12	33:17	7:48	8:19
5	39:37	42:15	7:55	8:27
6	48:09	51:22	8:01	8:33
7	56:47	1:00:34	8:06	8:39
8	1:05:31	1:09:53	8:11	8:44
9	1:14:19	1:19:16	8:15	8:48
10	1:23:11	1:28:44	8:19	8:52
11	1:32:07	1:38:15	8:22	8:55
12	1:41:06	1:47:50	8:25	8:59
13	1:50:08	1:57:29	8:28	9:02
14	1:59:14	2:07:11	8:31	9:05
15	2:08:22	2:16:55	8:33	9:07
16	2:17:33	2:26:43	8:35	9:10
17	2:26:46	2:36:33	8:38	9:12
18	2:36:01	2:46:25	8:40	9:14
19	2:45:19	2:56:20	8:42	9:16
20	2:54:38	3:06:17	8:43	9:18
21	3:04:00	3:16:16	8:45	9:20
22	3:13:23	3:26:17	8:47	9:22
23	3:22:49	3:36:20	8:49	9:24
24	3:32:16	3:46:25	8:50	9:26
25	3:41:44	3:56:31	8:52	9:27

Training Paces for 42 Minute 10K Runner

(3:16 Marathon Goal)

Marathon Goal Pace: 7:28 per mile

Max Aerobic Pace: 1:32 per 440 yds

Miles	Time	Easy Run Paces: (min)	Pace (min/mi)	
2	15:36	16:38	7:48	8:19
3	24:05	25:41	8:01	8:33
4	32:46	34:57	8:11	8:44
5	41:36	44:22	8:19	8:52
6	50:34	53:56	8:25	8:59
7	59:38	1:03:36	8:31	9:05
8	1:08:47	1:13:22	8:35	9:10
9	1:18:02	1:23:14	8:40	9:14
10	1:27:20	1:33:10	8:44	9:19
11	1:36:43	1:43:10	8:47	9:22
12	1:46:09	1:53:14	8:50	9:26
13	1:55:39	2:03:22	8:53	9:29
14	2:05:12	2:13:32	8:56	9:32
15	2:14:47	2:23:46	8:59	9:35
16	2:24:25	2:34:03	9:01	9:37
17	2:34:06	2:44:23	9:03	9:40
18	2:43:49	2:54:45	9:06	9:42
19	2:53:35	3:05:09	9:08	9:44
20	3:03:22	3:15:36	9:10	9:46
21	3:13:12	3:26:05	9:12	9:48
22	3:23:04	3:36:36	9:13	9:50
23	3:32:57	3:47:09	9:15	9:52
24	3:42:53	3:57:44	9:17	9:54
25	3:52:50	4:08:21	9:18	9:56

Training Paces for 44 Minute 10K Runner

(3:25 Marathon Goal)

Marathon Goal Pace: 7:49 per mile

Max Aerobic Pace: 1:36 per 440 yds

Miles	Time	Easy Run Paces: (min)	Pace(min/mi)	
2	16:21	17:26	8:10	8:43
3	25:14	26:54	8:24	8:58
4	34:19	36:37	8:34	9:09
5	43:35	46:29	8:43	9:17
6	52:58	56:30	8:49	9:25
7	1:02:28	1:06:38	8:55	9:31
8	1:12:04	1:16:52	9:00	9:36
9	1:21:45	1:27:12	9:05	9:41
10	1:31:30	1:37:36	9:09	9:45
11	1:41:19	1:48:05	9:12	9:49
12	1:51:13	1:58:38	9:16	9:53
13	2:01:09	2:09:14	9:19	9:56
14	2:11:09	2:19:54	9:22	9:59
15	2:21:12	2:30:37	9:24	10:02
16	2:31:18	2:41:23	9:27	10:05
17	2:41:26	2:52:12	9:29	10:07
18	2:51:37	3:03:04	9:32	10:10
19	3:01:51	3:13:58	9:34	10:12
20	3:12:06	3:24:55	9:36	10:14
21	3:22:24	3:35:54	9:38	10:16
22	3:32:44	3:46:55	9:40	10:18
23	3:43:06	3:57:58	9:42	10:20
24	3:53:29	4:09:03	9:43	10:22
25	4:03:55	4:20:11	9:45	10:24

Training Paces for 46 Minute 10K Runner

(3:34 Marathon Goal)

Marathon Goal Pace: 8:11 per mile

Max Aerobic Pace: 1:41 per 440 yds

Miles	Time	Easy Run Paces: (min)	Pace (min/mi)	
2	17:05	18:14	8:32	9:07
3	26:22	28:08	8:47	9:22
4	35:53	38:16	8:58	9:34
5	45:34	48:36	9:06	9:43
6	55:23	59:04	9:13	9:50
7	1:05:18	1:09:40	9:19	9:57
8	1:15:20	1:20:22	9:25	10:02
9	1:25:28	1:31:09	9:29	10:07
10	1:35:39	1:42:02	9:33	10:12
11	1:45:56	1:53:00	9:37	10:16
12	1:56:16	2:04:01	9:41	10:20
13	2:06:40	2:15:06	9:44	10:23
14	2:17:07	2:26:16	9:47	10:26
15	2:27:37	2:37:28	9:50	10:29
16	2:38:11	2:48:43	9:53	10:32
17	2:48:47	3:00:02	9:55	10:35
18	2:59:25	3:11:23	9:58	10:37
19	3:10:07	3:22:47	10:00	10:40
20	3:20:50	3:34:14	10:02	10:42
21	3:31:36	3:45:43	10:04	10:44
22	3:42:24	3:57:14	10:06	10:47
23	3:53:14	4:08:47	10:08	10:49
24	4:04:06	4:20:23	10:10	10:50
25	4:15:00	4:32:00	10:12	10:52

Training Paces for 48 Minute 10K Runner

(3:44 Marathon Goal)

Marathon Goal Pace: 8:32 per mile

Max Aerobic Pace: 1:45 per 440 yds

Miles	Time	Easy Run Paces: (min)	Pace(min/mi)	
2	17:50	19:01	8:55	9:30
3	27:31	29:21	9:10	9:47
4	37:26	39:56	9:21	9:59
5	47:32	50:43	9:30	10:08
6	57:47	1:01:38	9:37	10:16
7	1:08:09	1:12:41	9:44	10:23
8	1:18:37	1:23:51	9:49	10:28
9	1:29:10	1:35:07	9:54	10:34
10	1:39:49	1:46:28	9:58	10:38
11	1:50:32	1:57:54	10:02	10:43
12	2:01:19	2:09:25	10:06	10:47
13	2:12:10	2:20:59	10:10	10:50
14	2:23:05	2:32:37	10:13	10:54
15	2:34:02	2:44:19	10:16	10:57
16	2:45:03	2:56:04	10:18	11:00
17	2:56:07	3:07:52	10:21	11:03
18	3:07:14	3:19:43	10:24	11:05
19	3:18:23	3:31:36	10:26	11:08
20	3:29:34	3:43:33	10:28	11:10
21	3:40:48	3:55:31	10:30	11:12
22	3:52:04	4:07:33	10:32	11:15
23	4:03:23	4:19:36	10:34	11:17
24	4:14:43	4:31:42	10:36	11:19
25	4:26:05	4:43:50	10:38	11:21

Training Paces for 50 Minute 10K Runner

(3:53 Marathon Goal)

Marathon Goal Pace: 8:53 per mile

Max Aerobic Pace: 1:49 per 440 yds

Miles	Time	Easy Run Paces: (min)	Pace(min/mi)	
2	18:34	19:49	9:17	9:54
3	28:40	30:35	9:33	10:11
4	39:00	41:36	9:45	10:24
5	49:31	52:49	9:54	10:33
6	1:00:11	1:04:12	10:01	10:42
7	1:10:59	1:15:43	10:08	10:49
8	1:21:53	1:27:21	10:14	10:55
9	1:32:53	1:39:05	10:19	11:00
10	1:43:59	1:50:55	10:23	11:05
11	1:55:08	2:02:49	10:28	11:09
12	2:06:23	2:14:48	10:31	11:14
13	2:17:41	2:26:51	10:35	11:17
14	2:29:02	2:38:59	10:38	11:21
15	2:40:28	2:51:09	10:41	11:24
16	2:51:56	3:03:24	10:44	11:27
17	3:03:27	3:15:41	10:47	11:30
18	3:15:02	3:28:02	10:50	11:33
19	3:26:39	3:40:25	10:52	11:36
20	3:38:18	3:52:51	10:54	11:38
21	3:50:00	4:05:20	10:57	11:40
22	4:01:44	4:17:51	10:59	11:43
23	4:13:31	4:30:25	11:01	11:45
24	4:25:20	4:43:01	11:03	11:47
25	4:37:11	4:55:39	11:05	11:49

Training Paces for 52 Minute 10K Runner

(4:02 Marathon Goal)

Marathon Goal Pace: 9:15 per mile

Max Aerobic Pace: 1:54 per 440 yds

Easy Run Paces:

Miles	Time	(min)	Pace(min/mi)	
2	19:19	20:36	9:39	10:18
3	29:49	31:48	9:56	10:36
4	40:34	43:16	10:08	10:49
5	51:30	54:56	10:18	10:59
6	1:02:36	1:06:46	10:26	11:07
7	1:13:50	1:18:45	10:32	11:15
8	1:25:10	1:30:51	10:38	11:21
9	1:36:36	1:43:03	10:44	11:27
10	1:48:08	1:55:21	10:48	11:32
11	1:59:45	2:07:44	10:53	11:36
12	2:11:26	2:20:12	10:57	11:41
13	2:23:11	2:32:44	11:00	11:44
14	2:35:00	2:45:20	11:04	11:48
15	2:46:53	2:58:00	11:07	11:52
16	2:58:49	3:10:44	11:10	11:55
17	3:10:48	3:23:31	11:13	11:58
18	3:22:50	3:36:21	11:16	12:01
19	3:34:55	3:49:14	11:18	12:03
20	3:47:02	4:02:10	11:21	12:06
21	3:59:12	4:15:09	11:23	12:09
22	4:11:25	4:28:10	11:25	12:11
23	4:23:39	4:41:14	11:27	12:13
24	4:35:57	4:54:20	11:29	12:15
25	4:48:16	5:07:29	11:31	12:17

Training Paces for 54 Minute 10K Runner

(4:12 Marathon Goal)

Marathon Goal Pace: 9:36 per mile

Max Aerobic Pace: 1:58 per 440 yds

Miles	Time	Easy Run Paces: (min)	Pace (min/mi)	
2	20:04	21:24	10:02	10:42
3	30:58	33:01	10:19	11:00
4	42:07	44:56	10:31	11:14
5	53:29	57:03	10:41	11:24
6	1:05:00	1:09:21	10:50	11:33
7	1:16:40	1:21:47	10:57	11:41
8	1:28:27	1:34:20	11:03	11:47
9	1:40:19	1:47:01	11:08	11:53
10	1:52:18	1:59:47	11:13	11:58
11	2:04:21	2:12:39	11:18	12:03
12	2:16:29	2:25:35	11:22	12:07
13	2:28:42	2:38:36	11:26	12:12
14	2:40:58	2:51:42	11:29	12:15
15	2:53:18	3:04:51	11:33	12:19
16	3:05:41	3:18:04	11:36	12:22
17	3:18:08	3:31:21	11:39	12:25
18	3:30:38	3:44:40	11:42	12:28
19	3:43:11	3:58:03	11:44	12:31
20	3:55:46	4:11:29	11:47	12:34
21	4:08:24	4:24:58	11:49	12:37
22	4:21:05	4:38:29	11:52	12:39
23	4:33:48	4:52:03	11:54	12:41
24	4:46:33	5:05:40	11:56	12:44
25	4:59:21	5:19:18	11:58	12:46

Training Paces for 56 Minute 10K Runner

(4:21 Marathon Goal)

Marathon Goal Pace: 9:58 per mile

Max Aerobic Pace: 2:03 per 440 yds

Miles	Time	Easy Run Paces: (min)	Pace	(min/mi)
2	20:48	22:11	10:24	11:05
3	32:06	34:15	10:42	11:25
4	43:41	46:36	10:55	11:39
5	55:28	59:10	11:05	11:50
6	1:07:25	1:11:55	11:14	11:59
7	1:19:30	1:24:48	11:21	12:06
8	1:31:43	1:37:50	11:27	12:13
9	1:44:02	1:50:59	11:33	12:19
10	1:56:27	2:04:13	11:38	12:25
11	2:08:58	2:17:33	11:43	12:30
12	2:21:33	2:30:59	11:47	12:34
13	2:34:12	2:44:29	11:51	12:39
14	2:46:56	2:58:03	11:55	12:43
15	2:59:43	3:11:42	11:58	12:46
16	3:12:34	3:25:24	12:02	12:50
17	3:25:28	3:39:10	12:05	12:53
18	3:38:26	3:53:00	12:08	12:56
19	3:51:26	4:06:52	12:10	12:59
20	4:04:30	4:20:48	12:13	13:02
21	4:17:36	4:34:47	12:16	13:05
22	4:30:45	4:48:48	12:18	13:07
23	4:43:56	5:02:52	12:20	13:10
24	4:57:10	5:16:59	12:22	13:12
25	5:10:26	5:31:08	12:25	13:14

EXAMPLE 8 WEEK INTERVAL PROGRESSION

This is an 8 week strength training progression which could be used by an advanced marathoner during the sharpening phase of his training. These workouts are *not* recommended for beginning or intermediate marathoners.

The goal of this program is to increase anaerobic threshold and maximal oxygen uptake (VO2 max).

Workouts are to be done one per week on a *hard* workout day for 8 consecutive weeks. Each workout should consist of at least a 1 mile easy warmup run and some stretching followed by the intervals and then by a 2 or more mile cool down run.

During the recovery jog, monitor your pulse to see that it drops to 55 to 65% of your maximum heart rate before the next interval.

This progression increases from 6 to 12 440's during the 8 week period while the speed is slowly added until all the intervals are run at maximum aerobic pace. Maximum aerobic pace is given in the appendix training pace tables for 440 yd (400 meters). For 220 yd (200 meters), simply divide by 2. For 90% pace times, multiply the maximum aerobic pace time by 1.1. For example if your max aerobic pace (100%) time is 80 seconds for 440 yards, your 90% time is 88 seconds and your 90% 220 time is 44 seconds.

Interval Progression

Week 1:
- 4 x 220 yds at 90%, 110 yd recovery.
- 6 x 440 yds at 90%, 220 yd recovery.

Week 2:
- 4 x 220 yds at 90%, 110 yd recovery.
- 8 x 440 yds at 90%, 220 yd recovery.

Week 3:
- 2 x 220 yds at 90%, 110 yd recovery.
- 2 x 220 yds at 100%, 110 yd recovery.
- 2 x 440 yds at 100%, 220 yd recovery.
- 8 x 440 yds at 90%, 220 yd recovery.

Week 4:
- 2 x 220 yds at 90%, 110 yd recovery.
- 2 x 220 yds at 100%, 110 yd recovery.
- 4 x 440 yds at 100%, 220 yd recovery.
- 6 x 440 yds at 90%, 220 yd recovery.

Week 5:
- 2 x 220 yds at 90%, 110 yd recovery.
- 2 x 220 yds at 100%, 110 yd recovery.
- 6 x 440 yds at 100%, 220 yd recovery.
- 4 x 440 yds at 90%, 220 yd recovery.

Week 6:
- 2 x 220 yds at 90%, 110 yd recovery.
- 2 x 220 yds at 100%, 110 yd recovery.
- 8 x 440 yds at 100%, 220 yd recovery.
- 2 x 440 yds at 90%, 220 yd recovery.

Week 7:
- 2 x 220 yds at 90%, 110 yd recovery.
- 2 x 220 yds at 100%, 110 yd recovery.
- 10 x 440 yds at 100%, 220 yd recovery.

Week 8:
- 2 x 220 yds at 90%, 110 yd recovery.
- 2 x 220 yds at 100%, 110 yd recovery.
- 12 x 440 yds at 100%, 110 yd recovery.

EXAMPLE 8 WEEK REPEAT PROGRESSION

This is an 8 week pace and strength training progression which could be used by an intermediate or advanced marathoner during the sharpening phase of his training. This type of workout is *not* recommended for beginning marathoners. Intermediate marathoners could substitute this progression for a *Tempo Run* progression.

The goal of these workouts is to develop neuromuscular coordination and "speed sense" at marathon race pace. A side benefit is an increase in anaerobic threshold.

Workouts are to be done on a *hard* workout day one per week for 8 consecutive weeks. Each workout consists of at least a 1 mile easy warmup run and some stretching followed by the repeats and then a 2 or more mile easy cooldown run.

Between repeats, allow complete recovery to 50% of max heart rate or lower by jogging at a very slow pace for 1/2 the repeat distance or more.

The progression increases from 5 miles at 90% of marathon goal pace to 7 miles at 100% of marathon goal pace. Marathon goal paces are given in the appendix training pace tables. To determine a 90% goal pace multiply the appendix time/mile by 1.1. For example, if your marathon goal pace is 7 min/mile your 90% goal pace is 7.7 min/mile or 7:42.

1 Mile Repeat Progression

Week 1:
- 5 x 1 mile at 90% goal pace

Week 2:
- 6 x 1 mile at 90% goal pace

Week 3:
- 6 x 1 mile at 90% goal pace
- 1 x 1 mile at 100% goal pace

Week 4:
- 4 x 1 mile at 90% goal pace
- 3 x 1 mile at 100% goal pace

Week 5:
- 2 x 1 mile at 90% goal pace

- 5 x 1 mile at 100% goal pace

Week 6:
- 1 x 1 mile at 90% goal pace
- 7 x 1 mile at 100% goal pace

Week 7:
- 7 x 1 mile at 100% goal pace

Week 8:
- 7 x 1 mile at 100% goal pace

EXAMPLE 8 WEEK FARTLEK PROGRAM

This is an 8 week strength training progression which could be used by an intermediate or advanced marathoner during the sharpening phase of his training. These workouts are *not* recommended for beginning marathoners.

The goal of this program is to increase anerobic threshold and maximal oxygen uptake (VO2 max).

Workouts are to be done one per week on a *hard* workout day for 8 consecutive weeks. Each workout should consist of an easy warmup run followed by the fartlek and then by an easy cooldown run.

Fartlek is an unstructured workout, but the following guidelines should be used.

1. If possible run on a golf course, trail or other undulating terrain.

2. Keep the total length of the fartlek phase of the workout to less than 10% of your weekly mileage.

3. Run random distances between 50 yards and 1 mile at hard (90%) effort, with easy (75-80%) running in between until you feel that you have recovered.

4. Work the terrain. Charge some uphills. Stride some downhills. Try to use all your muscles.

5. Fartlek should be like "play".

Fartlek Progression

Week 1:
- 4 miles easy
- 3 miles fartlek
- 4 miles easy

Week 2:
- 2 miles easy
- 4 miles fartlek
- 2 miles easy

Week 3:
- 2 miles easy
- 5 miles fartlek
- 2 miles easy

Week 4:
- 2 miles easy
- 5-6 miles fartlek
- 2 miles easy

Week 5-8:
- 2 miles easy
- 6-7 miles fartlek *
- 2 miles easy

* Increase the intensity each week as you develop more strength.

EXAMPLE 8 WEEK HILL TRAINING PROGRESSION

This is an 8 week strength training progression which could be used by an advanced marathoner during the sharpening phase of his training. These workouts are *not* recommended for beginning or intermediate marathoners. They are *very stressful* and should be used with caution even by advanced runners.

The goal of this program is to increase anerobic

threshold and maximal oxygen uptake (VO2 max). Additional benefits include form enhancement and high speed running efficiency.

Workouts are to be done one per week on a *hard* workout day for 8 consecutive weeks. Each workout should consist of at least a 1 mile easy warmup run and some stretching followed by the hill repeats and then by a 2 or more mile cooldown run.

This progression increases from 3 to 8 hill repeats during the 8 week period.

Lay out a circuit, preferably on a golf course or some other soft surface, with a hill about 200 meters long having a flat runout on the top and bottom. The hill should be comfortable to run down, not too steep. Each hill repeat consists of the following:

1. Bound up the hill. This is not fast running, but more like the take off of a long jump, with exaggerated knee lift and arm swing. Go for height. It may take you 1 or 2 workouts to get the hang of it.

2. Jog a loop of 200 meters or so at the top of the hill to recover.

3. Stride down the hill and out onto the flat. Work on a fast long stride, paying attention to smooth upper and lower body movement.

4. Jog a loop of 200 meters or so back to the bottom of the hill to recover.

Hill Repeat Progression

Week 1:
- 3 hill repeats

Week 2:
- 4 hill repeats

Week 3:
- 5 hill repeats

Week 4:
- 6 hill repeats

Week 5:
- 7 hill repeats

Week 6-8
- 8 hill repeats

REFERENCES

Anderson, Tim & Kearney, J.T. "Effects of Three Resistance Training Programs on Muscular Strength and Absolute and Relative Endurance" *Research Quarterly for Exercise and Sport* (53:1) 1982, pp. 1-7.

Alter, Judy *Surviving Exercise* Houghten Mifflin Co. Boston, 1983.

Bandura, A. "Self-Reinforcement Process" in *Self-Control: Power to the Person* (M.J. Mahoney & C.E. Thoreson, eds.) Brooks/Cole Publishing Co., Monteray, Ca. 1974, pp. 86-110.

Bobbert, Maarten F, Hollander, A. P. & Huijing, P. A. "Factors in Delayed Onset Muscular Soreness of Man" *Medicine and Science in Sports and Exercise* (18:1) 1986, pp. 75-81.

Brody, Jane *Jane Brody's Nutrition Book* Bantam Books, New York, New York, 1982.

Coleman, Ellen *Eating For Endurance* Roubidoux Printing Co., Riverside Ca., 1980.

Costill, David L., Ph. D. *A Scientific Approach to Distance Running* Track & Field News, 1979.

Daniels, J., Fitts, R. & Sheehan, G. *Conditioning for Distance Running, The Scientific Aspects* John Wiley & Son, New York, 1978.

Daws, Ron *Running Your Best* The Stephen Greene Press, Lexington, Massachusetts, 1985.

Finke, P. "Back to Basics" Series in *The Oregon Distance Runner* Winter, Spring & Summer 1984.

Finke, P. "A Guide to Ultratraining" *Ultrarunning* (4:9) March 1985, pp. 22-25.

Forgac, M.T. "Carbohydrate Loading: A Review" *Journal of the American Dietetic Association* (75) July, 1979, pp. 42-45.

Garfield, Charles A., Ph.D. & Bennett, H.Z. *Peak Performance* Jeremy P. Tarcher, Inc., Los Angeles 1984.

Garfield, Charles A., Ph.D. "On Vitamins, Carboloading & Competition" *Womens Sports & Fitness* (7:9) October 1985.

Hartung, G.H. & Squires, W.G. "Physiologic Measures & Marathon Running Performance in Young & Middle Aged Runners" *Journal of Sports Medicine* (22) 1982, pp. 366-370.

Higdon, H. "Shadows on the Wall" *The Runner* November 1981, pp. 46, 50, 80-81.

Macek, M. & Vavia, J. "FIMS Position Statement on Training and Competition in Children" *The Journal of Sports Medicine and Physical Fitness* (20:2) 1980, pp 135-138.

McArdle, W.D., Katch, F.I. & Katch, V.L. *Exercise Physiology. Energy, Nutrition & Human Performance* Lea & Febiger, Philadelphia, 1981.

Millman, Dan *The Warrior Athlete : Body Mind & Spirit* Stillpoint Publishing, Walpole, New Hampshire 1979.

Moore, M. "Carbohydrate Loading: Eating through the Wall" *The Physician & Sportsmedicine* (9) October 1981, pp. 97-102.

Orlick, Terry *In Pursuit of Excellence* Human Kinetics Publishers, Champaign, Ill., 1982.

Overfield, J.H. "Marathoning's Glorious Birth" *Marathoner* Winter 1979, pp. 22-25.

Potera, Carol "The Running Body" *Running Times* November, 1985.

Reynolds, Bill *Weight Training for Beginners* Contemporary Books, Inc., Chicago, 1982.

Runner's Training Guide Runner's World Magazine, 1973.

Shetlock, Frank G. & Prentice, W. E. "Warming Up and Stretching for Improved Physical Performance and Prevention of Sports-Related Injuries" *Sports Medicine* (2) 1985, pp. 267-278.

Sjodin, Bertil & Svedenhag, J. "Applied Physiology of Marathon Running" *Sports Medicine* (2) 1985, pp. 83-99.

van der Beek, E. J. "Vitamins and Endurance Training" *Sports Medicine* (2) 1985, pp. 175-197.

Williams, M.H. *Nutrition for Fitness & Sport* Wm. C. Brown Company, Pubs. Dubuque, Iowa, 1983.

Wilmore, J.H. *Training for Sport & Activity. The Physiological Basis of the Conditioning Process* Allyn & Bacon, Inc., 1982.

Wischnia, B. "The Elements of Style" *Runner's World* December 1982, pp. 55-62.

Zimmer, Judith *Free Weights* Villard Books, New York, 1985.

INDEX

A
Abdominal strengthening 103
Abductor 117
Acclimatization 73
Adaptation 10-11, 15
   altitude 73
   cardiovascular 13
   heat 73
   respiratory 13
Adductor 117
   stretches 101
Adenosine triphosphate 11
Adequate
   base 26
   recovery 17
Adipose tissue 128
Advanced marathoner 29
   basebuilding 34
   recovery 93
   sharpening 49
   tapering 63
Aerobic
   enzymes 12
   maximum pace 42, 44
   metabolism 11
   power 44
Age 4
Aid 83
   stations 83
Aids to performance 95
Alcohol 139
Alanine 132
Altitude
   adaptation 73
   racing 73
American Academy of Pediatrics 4
Amino acids 130
   essential 131
Amphetamines 138
Anaerobic
   metabolism 11
   threshold 13
Animal fats 130
Ankle weights 107
Anxiety 50
Aspirin 140
Assessment, self 56
Atherosclerosis 129
Athletics West 22
ATP 11

B
Balanced diet 122
Ball State
   Human Performance Lab 64

Basebuilding 25-27
   advanced 34
   beginning 32
   intermediate 33
Bathrooms 77
Beginning marathoner 4
   basebuilding 32
   recovery 92
   sharpening 47
   tapering 61
Beginning training 28
Behavioral strategies 50
Belly breathing 53
Bench press 109
Benoit, Joan 51
Bent lateral raises 112
Biceps brachii 108
Black toe 76
Blood 13
   doping 140
   pressure drop 80
Body
   composition 13
   enzymes 132
   monitoring 17, 56
Boston Athletic Association II
Breathing deep 52-53
Brown, Dick 22
Building
   a base 25-27
   endurance 27
   mileage 18

C
Caffeine 139
Calcium 134
Cancer 130
Capillaries 13
Carbohydrate 11-12, 64, 124-125
   complex 65, 125
   loading 60, 64-66
   simple 65
Carbon dioxide 11
Cardiovascular
   endurance 27
   adaptations 13
Certified course 81
Chafing 77
Checklist for marathon 72
Children 4
Cholesterol 128
Circuit 106
Circuit weight training 106
   exercises 121
   programs 121
   progressions 121
   schedule 121

Clinics 17, 23
Clothing for race 76
CO2 11
Coaches 17
Coaching 23
Cold 142
    temperature running 149
Commitment 5, 35
Common questions 22
Complex carbohydrates 65, 125
Concentration 53
    cycles 53
Connective tissue 27
Convertible muscle 12, 40
Cool-down 31, 80
Coordination, neuromuscular 41
Core temperature 143
Corners cutting 81
Coronary
    heart disease 128
    risk factors 129
Costill, David 64
Cough 22
Course
    certification 81
    knowledge 69-70
Cramps muscle 84
Cross training 43
Curl downs 105
Curl ups 104
Curls 116
Cutting corners 81
Cycles, concentration 53

D

Daily mileage ratios 28, 30
Date pace 45
Davies, Clive 4
De Coubertin, Baron Pierre I
Dealing with discomfort 57
Deep breathing 52-53
Deltoid 108
Depletion 64, 89
Diabetics 66
Diaphragmatic breathing 53
Diarrhea 65
Diary 21
Discomfort, dealing with 57
Distance 19
Double workouts 31
Drafting 82-83
Drinking aid 83
Dumbbell 107
    flys 110

E

Easy 19-20, 27
    workout 16
Effort, even 43, 69

Electrolyte 135
    balance 135
    loss 143
    replacement 89
Endurance
    base 26
    cardiovascular 27
    increasing 27
    training 13, 40
    weight training 106
Energy
    sources 11
    store replenishment 90
Enzymes, oxidative 60
Equipment checklist 72
Ergogenic aids 137
Even effort 43, 69

F

Fartlek 41, 46
    workout example 173-174
Fat 11-12, 127
    animal 130
    metabolism 40
    saturated 128
    stores 12
    unsaturated 128
Fatigue
    long term 91
    post race 89
Fatty acids 127
Final sharpening 60
Finish
    goals 67-68
    location 77
Finishing 80
Flexibility 96
    individual differences 98
Fluid 81, 137
    intake 136
    loss 143
    replacement drinks 137, 148
Focus 53, 55
Food
    and performance 122
    groups 123
Free fatty acids 130

G

Gastrocnemius stretches 100
Glucose
    during exercise 126
    solutions 127
Glycogen 11-12, 64, 125
Goal 55
    finish 67
    pace 45
    race pace 41
    setting 5
Golgi tendons 97

H

H_2O 11
Habit 35
Hamstring 117
    stretches 99
Hard 19-20, 27
    workout 16
Hard/easy 10, 28
    cycles 15
HDL 129
Headwinds 82
Heart 13
    rate 29
    rate maximum 42
    rate recovery 21
    rate resting 21
    rate training 29
Heat 142
    acclimatization 143, 145
    acclimatization techniques 146-147
    adaptation 73
    cramps 143
    exhaustion 144
    illness 143
    stroke 144
Heredity 13
Hill training 42
    workout example 174-176
Hills, racing on 69
Hip flexor stretches 101
Hitting the wall 12
Hold-relax stretching 98
Hot climate racing 73
Hot tub 81
HR 21
Human modeling 51
Humidity 143-144
Hyperhydration 138
Hypoglycemia 127

I

Ice 80, 89
Igloi, Mihaly 43
Imagery 52, 57
    mental 52
Inadequate nutrition 122
Increasing mileage 30
Injury 36
    minor recovery 60
    prevention 15, 17
Insulin reaction 65
Intermediate marathoner
    basebuilding 33
    recovery 92
    sharpening 48
    tapering 62
Intervals 42
    training 43
    workout example 170-171
Intestinal cramps 138
Iron 134

K

Knowledge of course 69-70

L

Lactic acid 11, 13
Latissimus dorsi 108
Layered clothing 149
LDL 129
Leg
    curls 119
    extensions 118
    flexions 119
Lipids 127
Loading, carbohydrate 60, 64-66
Location of finish 77
Long runs 29-30
Lopes, Carlos 4, 51
Loues, Spiridon I
Low back pain 102
Low temperature running 149
Lower body weights 117

M

Marathon I
    checklist 72
    length II
    metabolism 12

    potential 67
Marathoning
    for children 4
    for older runners 4
    for women 4
Maximizing performance 40
Maximum aerobic pace 42, 44
Maximum heart rate 42
Medical problems 4
Mental imagery 52
Metabolism 12
    fat 40
Mileage
    daily ratios 28, 30
    increasing 18, 30
    progressions 29-30
    weekly 26
Minerals 134
Mission 6
Mitochondria 12
Modeling 51
    human 51
Monitoring, body 17, 21, 56
Motivation 5, 35
Muscle
    convertible 12, 40
    cramps 84
    glycogen 126
    soreness 88
    spasm 88

N

National Running Data Center 81

Nausea 80
Nautilus 107
Negative splits 68
Neuromuscular coordination 41
No pain no gain 22
Nutrient store rebuilding 60
Nutrition 122

O
Older runners 4
Olympics I
Overcompensation 15
Overload 10, 15
Overtraining 22
   signs 22
Oxidative enzymes 60
Oxygen 11-12
   consumption 12-13

P
Pace 29
   date 45
   goal 45
   judgement 41
   maximum aerobic 42
   maximum aerobic 44
   race goal 41
   tables 154-169
   training 29, 41
Pain relief 89
Peaking 55
   psychological 55
Pectoralis major 107
Pelvic tilts 103
Performance
   aids 95
   maximizing 40
Phases of training 26
Physiology 10
Plan 6
Planning a race 67, 71
Portland Marathon Clinic II
Positive splits 68
Post race
   fatigue 89
   workouts 91
Predicting times 67
Premack Principle 36
Preparation
   for race 59
   psychological 50
Prerace
   rest 73
   stretching 78
Proprioceptive neuromuscular
   facilitation 98
Protein 130-131
Psychological
   peaking 55
   preparation 50
Pyruvate 11

Q
Quadriceps 117
Questions common 22

R
Race
   dress 76
   morning 76
   number 76
   pace 41
   planning 67, 71
   preparation 26, 59
   recovery 21

   seeding 79
   specific training 46
   strategies 67
   tactics 81
Racing 31, 75
   first 10 miles 79
   last 6 miles 80
   second 10 miles 79
Rational strategies 50
Reaction, insulin 65
Rebuilding
   minor injuries 60
   nutrient stores 60
Recommended food servings 123
Recovery 15-16, 20, 87
   adequate 17
   advanced 93
   after marathon 89
   beginning 92
   day after marathon 89-90
   factors 88
   heart rate 21
   intermediate 92
   matrix 20
   month after marathon 91
   progressions 91
   race 21
   week after marathon 90-91
References 177-179
Relaxation 52, 56
Repeats 42, 45
   workout example 171-173
Repetition, circuit training 106
Repetitions 42
Replacement solutions 127
Resistance wind 82
Respiratory adaptations 13
Rest 15
   prerace 73
   heart rate 21
   HR increase 22
Rewards 35
Running
   in cold 149
   in heat 144-145
   in temperature extremes 142
Runs, tempo 44-45

S

Saturated fats 128
Schedule weekly 28
Seeding 79
Self
  assessment 56
  monitoring 21
  talk 56
  control 50
  reinforcement 50
Separating speed and distance 17, 19
Set 106
Sharpening 26, 39-40
  advanced 49
  beginning 47
  final 60
  intermediate 48
  programs 46
Shoes 76
Sickness 36
Side lateral raises 111
Side leg raises 120
Signs of overtraining 22
Simple carbohydrates 65
Simulation 51, 55-57
Single arm dumbbell rowing 114
Sluggishness 22
Soft surfaces 22
Soleus stretches 100
Sore throat 22
Soreness muscle 88
Spasm muscle 88
Specific workouts 19
Specificity 11, 15-16
Speed 19
  distance combinations 20
  play 41
  work 41
Spindles 97
Splits 68
  negative 68
  on hills 69
  positive 68
Spotter 109
Starting 78
Starting out 3
Steroids 138
Strategies
  behavioral 50
  race 67
  rational 50
Strength training 41
Stretch reflex 97
Stretches
  adductor 101
  back of thighs 99
  calves 100
  gastrocnemius 100
  hamstring 99
  hip flexor 101
  lower back 98
  soleus 100
Stretching 31, 96
  hold-relax method 98
  before running 97
  prerace 78
Stroke volume 13
Sugar
  before exercise 126
  simple 65
Super circuit training 107
Supercompensation 64
Supplemental training 96
Surfaces running 22
Swelling 81

T

Tactics, race 81
Taking aid 83
Talk test 29
Tapering 60
  advanced 63
  beginning 61
  intermediate 62
Temperature 142
Tempo runs 42, 44-45
Tendons, Golgi 97
Thirst 22
Time trial 42
Tired feeling 22
Training 28
  cross 43
  diary 21
  economy 15
  effect 15
  endurance 40
  for pace 41
  heart rate 29
  interval 43
  log 152
  log example 153
  on hills 42
  pace 29
  pace tables 154-169
  phases 26
  plan 6, 17-18
  principles 9
  race specific 46
  strength 41
  supplemental 96
  tempo runs 44-45
Trapezius 108
Triceps 108
  dumbbell press 113
  kickouts 115
Triglycerides 127

U

U.S. dietary goals 123, 125
U.S.D.A. dietary recommendations 124

Universal 107
Unsaturated fats 128
Upper body weights 107

V
Variety 36
Vaseline 77
Visualization 52, 56
Vitamins 132-133
    megadoses 134
    natural vs synthetic 133
VLDL 129
VO2 Max 13, 44
Volition 6

W
Wall 12
Warm-up 31, 77
Waste products 11
    flushing 89
Water 135-137
Weekly
    mileage 26
    schedule 28
Weggenman, Jim 98
Weight 106
Weight loss 22
Weight training
    endurance 106
    lower body 117
    upper body 107
Williams, Bob II
Willpower 6
Wind resistance 82
Women 4
Workouts
    double 31
    easy 19-20, 27
    hard 16, 19-20, 27